Practice*Planner*

Arthur E. Jongsma, Jr., Series Editor

Helping therapists help their clients...

Over 250,000 Practice*Planners*® sold ...

TheraScribe®

The Treatment Planning and Clinical Record Management System for Mental Health Professionals.

TheraScribe®—the latest version of our popular treatment planning, patient record-keeping software. Facilitates intake/assessment reporting, progress monitoring, and outcomes analysis. Supports group treatment and multiprovider treatment teams. Compatible with our full array of **PracticePlanners®** libraries, including our *Treatment Planner* software versions.

- This bestselling, easy-to-use Windows®-based software allows you to generate fully customized psychotherapy treatment plans that meet the requirements of all major accrediting agencies and most third-party payers.

- In just minutes, this user-friendly program's on-screen help enables you to create customized treatment plans.

- Praised in the *National Psychologist* and *Medical Software Reviews,* this innovative software simplifies and streamlines record-keeping.

- Available for a single user, or in a network version, this comprehensive software package suits the needs of all practices—both large and small.

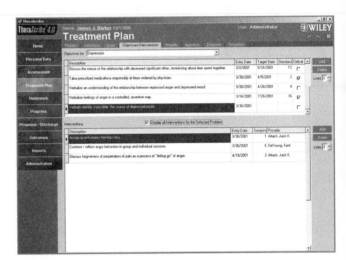

Treatment Planner Upgrade to Thera*Scribe*®

The behavioral definitions, goals, objectives, and interventions from this *Treatment Planner* can be imported into Thera*Scribe*®. For purchase and pricing information, please send in the coupon below or call 1-866-888-5158 or e-mail us at planners@wiley.com.

For more information about **TheraScribe**® or the Upgrade to this *Treatment Planner,* fill in this coupon and mail it to: R. Crucitt, John Wiley & Sons, Inc., 7222 Commerce Center Dr., Ste. 240, Colorado Springs, CO 80919 or e-mail us at planners@wiley.com.

❏ Please send me information on **TheraScribe**®

❏ Please send me information on the *Treatment Planner* Upgrade to **TheraScribe**®
   Name of *Treatment Planner* _____

❏ Please send me information on the network version of **TheraScribe**®

Name _____

Affiliation _____

Address _____

City/State/Zip _____

Phone _____ E-mail _____

For a free demo, visit us on the web at: therascribe.wiley.com

WILEY

Treatment Planners cover all the necessary elements for developing formal treatment plans, including detailed problem definitions, long-term goals, short-term objectives, therapeutic interventions, and DSM-IV™ diagnoses.

❏ **The Complete Adult Psychotherapy Treatment Planner,** Second Edition
    0-471-31924-4 / $49.95

❏ **The Child Psychotherapy Treatment Planner,** Second Edition
    0-471-34764-7 / $49.95

❏ **The Adolescent Psychotherapy Treatment Planner,** Second Edition
    0-471-34766-3 / $49.95

❏ **The Addiction Treatment Planner,** Second Edition
    0-471-41814-5 / $49.95

❏ **The Couples Psychotherapy Treatment Planner**
    0-471-24711-1 / $49.95

❏ **The Group Therapy Treatment Planner**
    0-471-37449-0 / $49.95

❏ **The Family Therapy Treatment Planner**
    0-471-34768-X / $49.95

❏ **The Older Adult Psychotherapy Treatment Planner**
    0-471-29574-4 / $49.95

❏ **The Employee Assistance (EAP) Treatment Planner**
    0-471-24709-X / $49.95

❏ **The Gay and Lesbian Psychotherapy Treatment Planner**
    0-471-35080-X / $49.95

❏ **The Crisis Counseling and Traumatic Events Treatment Planner**
    0-471-39587-0 / $49.95

❏ **The Social Work and Human Services Treatment Planner**
    0-471-37741-4 / $49.95

❏ **The Continuum of Care Treatment Planner**
    0-471-19568-5 / $49.95

❏ **The Behavioral Medicine Treatment Planner**
    0-471-31923-6 / $49.95

❏ **The Mental Retardation and Developmental Disability Treatment Planner**
    0-471-38253-1 / $49.95

❏ **The Special Education Treatment Planner**
    0-471-38872-6 / $49.95

❏ **The Severe and Persistent Mental Illness Treatment Planner**
    0-471-35945-9 / $49.95

❏ **The Personality Disorders Treatment Planner**
    0-471-39403-3 / $49.95

❏ **The Rehabilitation Psychology Treatment Planner**
    0-471-35178-4 / $49.95

❏ **The Pastoral Counseling Treatment Planner**
    0-471-25416-9 / $49.95

❏ **The Juvenile Justice and Residential Care Treatment Planner**
    0-471-43320-9 / $49.95

❏ **The Probation and Parole Treatment Planner**
    0-471-20244-4 / $49.95 (available 3/03)

❏ **The School Counseling and School Social Work Treatment Planner**
    0-471-08496-4 / $49.95

❏ **The Sexual Abuse Victim/Offender Treatment Planner**
    0-471-21979-7 / $49.95

Progress Notes Planners contain complete prewritten progress notes for each presenting problem in the companion Treatment Planners.

❏ **The Adult Psychotherapy Progress Notes Planner**
    0-471-34763-9 / $49.95

❏ **The Adolescent Psychotherapy Progress Notes Planner**
    0-471-38104-7 / $49.95

❏ **The Child Psychotherapy Progress Notes Planner**
    0-471-38102-0 / $49.95

❏ **The Addiction Progress Notes Planner**
    0-471-10330-6 / $49.95

❏ **The Severe and Persistent Mental Illness Progress Notes Planner**
    0-471-21986-X / $49.95

Name_____

Affiliation_____

Address_____

City/State/Zip_____

Phone/Fax_____

E-mail_____

On the web: practiceplanners.wiley.com

To order, call 1-800-225-5945
(Please refer to promo #1-4019 when ordering.)

Or send this page with payment* to:
John Wiley & Sons, Inc., Attn: J. Knott
111 River Street, Hoboken, NJ 07030

❏ Check enclosed   ❏ Visa   ❏ MasterCard   ❏ American Express

Card #_____

Expiration Date_____

Signature_____

*Please add your local sales tax to all orders.

Practice Management Tools for Busy Mental Health Professionals

Homework Planners feature dozens of behaviorally based, ready-to-use assignments that are designed for use between sessions, as well as a disk (Microsoft Word) containing all of the assignments—allowing you to customize them to suit your unique client needs.

☐ **Brief Therapy Homework Planner**
   0-471-24611-5 / $49.95

☐ **Brief Couples Therapy Homework Planner**
   0-471-29511-6 / $49.95

☐ **Brief Child Therapy Homework Planner**
   0-471-32366-7 / $49.95

☐ **Brief Adolescent Therapy Homework Planner**
   0-471-34465-6 / $49.95

☐ **Chemical Dependence Treatment Homework Planner**
   0-471-32452-3 / $49.95

☐ **Brief Employee Assistance Homework Planner**
   0-471-38088-1 / $49.95

☐ **Brief Family Therapy Homework Planner**
   0-471-385123-1 / $49.95

☐ **Grief Counseling Homework Planner**
   0-471-43318-7 / $49.95

☐ **Divorce Counseling Homework Planner**
   0-471-43319-5 / $49.95

☐ **Group Therapy Homework Planner**
   0-471-41822-6 / $49.95

☐ **The School Counseling and School Social Work Homework Planner**
   0-471-09114-6 / $49.95

Documentation Sourcebooks provide a comprehensive collection of ready-to-use blank forms, handouts, and questionnaires to help you manage your client reports and streamline the record keeping and treatment process. Features clear, concise explanations of the purpose of each form—including when it should be used and at what point. Includes customizable forms on disk.

☐ **The Clinical Documentation Sourcebook,**
   Second Edition
   0-471-32692-5 / $49.95

☐ **The Psychotherapy Documentation Primer**
   0-471-28990-6 / $45.00

☐ **The Couple and Family Clinical Documentation Sourcebook**
   0-471-25234-4 / $49.95

☐ **The Clinical Child Documentation Sourcebook**
   0-471-29111-0 / $49.95

☐ **The Chemical Dependence Treatment Documentation Sourcebook**
   0-471-31285-1 / $49.95

☐ **The Forensic Documentation Sourcebook**
   0-471-25459-2 / $95.00

☐ **The Continuum of Care Clinical Documentation Sourcebook**
   0-471-34581-4 / $85.00

To order by phone, call TOLL FREE 1-800-225-5945

Or contact us at:
John Wiley & Sons, Inc., Attn: J. Knott
111 River Street, Hoboken, NJ 07030
Fax: 1-800-597-3299
Online: www.practiceplanners.wiley.com

Child Therapy Activity and Homework Planner

PRACTICE*PLANNER*® SERIES

Treatment *Planners*

The Complete Adult Psychotherapy Treatment Planner, 2e
The Child Psychotherapy Treatment Planner, 2e
The Adolescent Psychotherapy Treatment Planner, 2e
The Continuum of Care Treatment Planner
The Couples Psychotherapy Treatment Planner
The Employee Assistance Treatment Planner
The Pastoral Counseling Treatment Planner
The Older Adult Psychotherapy Treatment Planner
The Behavioral Medicine Treatment Planner
The Group Therapy Treatment Planner
The Gay and Lesbian Psychotherapy Treatment Planner
The Family Therapy Treatment Planner
The Severe and Persistent Mental Illness Treatment Planner
The Mental Retardation and Developmental Disability Treatment Planner
The Social Work and Human Services Treatment Planner
The Crisis Counseling and Traumatic Events Treatment Planner
The Personality Disorders Treatment Planner
The Rehabilitation Psychology Treatment Planner
The Addiction Treatment Planner, 2e
The Special Education Treatment Planner
The Juvenile Justice and Residential Care Treatment Planner
The School Counseling and School Social Work Treatment Planner

Progress Notes *Planners*

The Child Psychotherapy Progress Notes Planner
The Adolescent Psychotherapy Progress Notes Planner
The Adult Psychotherapy Progress Notes Planner
The Addiction Progress Notes Planner
The Severe and Persistent Mental Illness Progress Notes Planner

Homework *Planners*

Brief Therapy Homework Planner
Brief Couples Therapy Homework Planner
Chemical Dependence Treatment Homework Planner
Brief Child Therapy Homework Planner
Brief Adolescent Therapy Homework Planner
Brief Employee Assistance Homework Planner
Brief Family Therapy Homework Planner
Grief Counseling Homework Planner
Group Therapy Homework Planner
Divorce Counseling Homework Planner
School Counseling and School Social Work Homework Planner
Child Therapy Activity and Homework Planner

Documentation *Sourcebooks*

The Clinical Documentation Sourcebook
The Forensic Documentation Sourcebook
The Psychotherapy Documentation Primer
The Chemical Dependence Treatment Documentation Sourcebook
The Clinical Child Documentation Sourcebook
The Couple and Family Clinical Documentation Sourcebook
The Clinical Documentation Sourcebook, 2e
The Continuum of Care Clinical Documentation Sourcebook

Practice*Planners*®

Arthur E. Jongsma, Jr., Series Editor

Child Therapy Activity and Homework Planner

Natalie Sufler Bilynsky

JOHN WILEY & SONS, INC.

Library of Congress Cataloging-in-Publication Data:

Bilynsky, Natalie Sufler.
    Child therapy activity and homework planner / Natalie Sufler Bilynsky.
        p. cm.—(Practice planners series)
    ISBN 0-471-25684-6
    1. Child psychotherapy. 2. Child psychotherapy—Problems, exercises, etc. I. Title. II. Practice planners.
    RJ504 .B557 2003
    618.92′8914—dc21   2002012717

Printed in the United States of America

10 9 8 7 6 5 4 3 2 1

This book is dedicated to my wonderful husband and loving family, for their endless support. Also, special thanks to all the children with whom I have worked, for their inspiration.

CONTENTS

PRACTICE*PLANNER*® SERIES PREFACE

The practice of psychotherapy has a dimension that did not exist 30, 20, or even 15 years ago—accountability. Treatment programs, public agencies, clinics, and even group and solo practitioners must now justify the treatment of patients to outside review entities that control the payment of fees. This development has resulted in an explosion of paperwork.

Clinicians must now document what has been done in treatment, what is planned for the future, and what the anticipated outcomes of the interventions are. The books and software in this Practice*Planner* series are designed to help practitioners fulfill these documentation requirements efficiently and professionally.

The Practice*Planner* series is growing rapidly. It now includes not only the original *Complete Adult Psychotherapy Treatment Planner, 2e,* the *Child Psychotherapy Treatment Planner, 2e,* and the *Adolescent Psychotherapy Treatment Planner, 2e,* but also *Treatment Planners* targeted to specialty areas of practice, including: addictions, the continuum of care, couples therapy, employee assistance, behavioral medicine, therapy with older adults, pastoral counseling, family therapy, group therapy, neuropsychology, therapy with gays and lesbians, and more.

In addition to the *Treatment Planners,* the series also includes Thera*Scribe*®, the latest version of the popular treatment planning, clinical record-keeping software, as well as adjunctive books—such as the *Brief, Chemical Dependence, Couples, Child, Adolescent, Family, Divorce,* and *Grief Therapy Homework Planners, The Psychotherapy Documentation Primer,* and *Clinical, Forensic, Child, Couples and Family, Continuum of Care,* and *Chemical Dependence Documentation Sourcebooks*—containing forms and resources to aid in mental health practice management. The goal of the series is to provide practitioners with the resources they need in order to provide high-quality care in the era of accountability—or, to put it simply, we seek to help you spend more time on patients, and less time on paperwork.

ARTHUR E. JONGSMA, JR.
Grand Rapids, Michigan

INTRODUCTION

Utilizing therapeutic exercises has two major advantages when providing mental health services to children. First, children are familiar with worksheets and often feel comfortable completing structured exercises. Children are frequently required to complete worksheets and structured activities in school. Therefore, the worksheets provide a familiar structure for working on complex issues that might otherwise seem overwhelming to the child. Second, children may be apprehensive and uncomfortable talking about an emotionally sensitive issue but able to draw a picture or write about this issue. Therapeutic work with children frequently involves drawing and planning activities that can help the child express him/herself. In fact, children are sometimes more able to write or draw a response that they would have difficulty verbalizing. Issues that are addressed in therapeutic exercises can then be focused upon in the therapy session.

Despite the fact that psychologists and other mental health professionals use exercises and drawings in therapy sessions, there is no comprehensive therapeutic activity book available for mental health professionals who work with young children. This therapeutic activity book is organized around specific presenting problems and provides a comprehensive guide for clinicians working with young children.

The *Child Therapy Activity and Homework Planner* is designed as a resource for the mental health professional with training and experience working with children. This book was organized based on *The Child Psychotherapy Treatment Planner, 2e* (Jongsma, Peterson, and McInnis, 2000), with each exercise corresponding to presenting problems listed in the *The Child Psychotherapy Treatment Planner*.

The assignments were not developed to adhere to specific theoretical orientation; instead, the therapeutic activities use methods based on various theoretical orientations and focus on specific clinical issues and presenting problems. Therefore, it is important for the clinician to carefully review each exercise to determine whether it matches the current focus of treatment.

HOW TO USE THE ACTIVITY AND HOMEWORK PLANNER

In preparing to use a specific exercise in a therapy session or as part of a homework assignment, review the entire therapeutic activity. Review the goals of the exercise and specific strategies suggested. Feel free to make changes in the exercise to make it more appropriate for the specific child and/or family with whom you are working.

In order to use the exercises most effectively, it is recommended that you review the entire workbook to get an overview of the scope and types of therapeutic activities presented. There may be multiple therapeutic exercises suggested for each presenting problem. Therefore, you can choose among the multiple therapeutic exercises suggested to address the child's treatment goals. Also, a series of activities can be combined to create a workbook focusing on clinically relevant topics. Although the therapeutic activities are divided into specific presenting problems, you can utilize worksheets from different sections to create a workbook that is unique for the child, choosing the worksheets deemed most helpful in dealing with the specific issues. For example, when working with a child coping with a recent loss, several therapeutic activities might be included, focusing on loss, feelings (anger and sadness), and problem solving.

It is important to note that the *Child Therapy Activity and Homework Planner* is designed for mental health professionals, psychologists, psychiatrists, social workers, and other professionals with training in providing therapy for children and families. This is not a self-help book for parents, but a resource for mental health professionals to aid in their therapeutic work with children.

FORMAT OF THE ASSIGNMENTS

The exercises compiled in this book are designed to be used in the therapy session, as homework, or as a combination of both, where the exercise is started in the therapy session and completed as homework.

As all work with children, some of the therapeutic exercises are designed specifically for the child, others for the parents/guardian, and some are to be completed with the child and parents/guardian together. Each therapeutic exercise includes specific instructions that indicate for whom the exercise was created.

To aid the clinician, each exercise begins with instructions for the therapist and suggestions for ways to use the exercise. Each therapeutic activity lists goals of the exercise and additional exercises that may be applicable to the presenting problem. In addition, there are suggestions about how to utilize the specific therapeutic activities.

It is a working assumption of the author that the mental health professional will use his/her best clinical judgment in determining the appropriateness of each assignment and the pace for completing the exercise. Certainly there will be situations where best clinical judgment would indicate that a single exercise be completed over several weeks. Similarly, there are many clinical issues that are so acute or sensitive that you, the mental health clinician, may determine that the exercise should only be completed within the therapy session, with ample time to process the emotionally sensitive material.

In preparing to use a specific assignment, review the exercise in its entirety prior to the therapy session. Reproduce necessary sections to complete the therapeutic exercise in the therapy session or as homework. Review the "Goals of the Exercise" and the "Suggestions for Processing This Exercise with Client" sections carefully. There may be exercises that require multiple copies or additional supplies (for example, pencils, crayons) to complete the exercise.

All of the exercises are included on the CD-ROM and can be reformatted to suit the specific needs of your client. For example, font size or the space to write a response can be increased for young children.

Clinical work with children is enhanced by the creativity of the therapist. Each exercise can be adapted for the individual client based on the clinical judgment of the therapist and dependent on the needs of the client. Therefore, you are encouraged to adapt the therapeutic exercise so it better fits the individual needs of the child. Additionally, completion of a specific exercise may result in additional areas upon which treatment should focus and create new therapeutic activities.

When explaining the exercise to the child and/or parents/guardian, be certain to explicitly state directions. Concretely describe the task and review the instructions several times to be certain that the child understands the therapeutic exercises.

When describing the therapeutic activity to the child, be certain that the instructions are in language that is age appropriate. In most situations it may be helpful to have the child repeat the directions for the exercise, particularly if this is a homework assignment.

If the child is to complete a therapeutic exercise with his/her parents'/guardian's assistance, be sure to review the instructions with everyone involved in the exercise.

For every homework assignment be sure to review the completed exercise in the next therapy session. Remind the child to bring the completed assignment to the next therapy session. When the therapeutic exercise is completed and reviewed, additional assignments can be considered to further aid the child.

It is my hope that the *Child Therapy Activity and Homework Planner* will help you in your therapeutic work with children and become a widely used tool in your clinical practice.

NATALIE SUFLER BILYNSKY, PH.D.

ACADEMIC ACHIEVEMENT

SCHOOL COMMUNICATION

GOALS OF THE EXERCISE

1. Develop strategies to help the child complete homework assignments on a regular basis.
2. Encourage parents/guardian to maintain regular communication with teachers.
3. Assist parents/guardian and teachers in development of a collaborative relationship.
4. Encourage parents/guardian to work with the school to improve the child's on-task behavior.

ADDITIONAL HOMEWORK THAT MAY BE APPLICABLE TO ACADEMIC ACHIEVEMENT

• ADHD	Establishing Behavioral Plans	Page 70
• Self-Esteem	Goal Setting	Page 313
• School Refusal	I'm Going to School	Page 273
• School Refusal	Positively School	Page 277
• School Refusal	School in View	Page 281

ADDITIONAL PROBLEMS FOR WHICH THIS EXERCISE MAY BE USEFUL

*   ADHD
*   Conduct Disorder
*   Disruptive Behavior
*   Oppositional Defiant Disorder
*   Peer Conflict
*   School Refusal

SUGGESTIONS FOR PROCESSING THIS EXERCISE WITH CLIENT

Children's academic and behavioral difficulties in school are often exacerbated by poor communication between teachers and parents/guardian. A primary goal in therapy is to improve communication between school staff and parents/guardian. Frequently parents/guardian report that they were unaware of school problems until they received report cards or notification of severe behavioral difficulties. Discussion about problem behaviors can become conflictual when family and school are placed in adversarial positions.

Parents/guardian frequently interpret comments from school administrators as personal attacks. This type of adversarial relationship can be avoided through improved communication between the school and home.

Although improving communication between the school and the family may seem like a simple task, it is important to remember that these relationships exist in a context. Families may become anxious and apprehensive in the school and resistant to any direct feedback. Comments from schools are often interpreted as judgmental and negative.

This assignment focuses on developing better communication between the classroom teacher and the primary caregiver. The therapist should review the daily report form with the parents/guardian who will discuss this form with the classroom teacher. The form is used to get a written report of the child's academic and/or behavioral performance for each day of the week. The teacher and parents/guardian also can communicate on a daily basis about the child's progress. Frequently parents/guardian and teachers communicate about negative incidents but do not focus on strategies that have been successful. This structured tool for regular communication between parents/guardian and school can be used to identify positive accomplishments.

In the therapy session, review the daily report sheet with parents/guardian. Show them that there is space for each day for the teacher to indicate behavior and a section for comments. The parents/guardian should schedule a brief meeting with the teacher to describe the daily report form. Any reservations about communication with the teacher should be addressed in the therapy session.

The parents/guardian and teacher should agree on a location for the behavior sheet (most typically, one of the child's notebooks). The daily report sheet should also be explained to the child in concrete terms: "Each day your teacher will be letting Mom and Dad know about your behavior in school. When you come home from school Mom and Dad will review the daily report and sign it."

The family can also establish a reward system related to classroom behavior. For example, if there are stars for both morning (a.m.) and afternoon (p.m.) behavior for the day, the child can watch a favorite television program after school.

SCHOOL COMMUNICATION

Please complete the following daily report for _____

Date: _____

	Monday	Tuesday	Wednesday	Thursday	Friday
Classroom behavior a.m.					
Classroom behavior p.m.					
Completion of assignments					
Comments					
Teacher's signature					
Parent's/guardian's comments					
Parent's/guardian's signature					

SCHOOL IS OKAY

GOALS OF THE EXERCISE

1. Reinforce the client's successful school experience and positive statements about school.
2. Encourage positive statements about school and academic ability.

ADDITIONAL HOMEWORK THAT MAY BE APPLICABLE TO ACADEMIC ACHIEVEMENT

- ADHD   Establishing Behavioral Plans   Page 70
- Self-Esteem   Goal Setting   Page 313
- School Refusal   I'm Going to School   Page 273
- School Refusal   Positively School   Page 277
- School Refusal   School in View   Page 281

ADDITIONAL PROBLEMS FOR WHICH THIS EXERCISE MAY BE USEFUL

- ADHD
- Conduct Disorder
- Disruptive Behavior
- Oppositional Defiant Disorder
- Peer Conflict
- School Refusal

SUGGESTIONS FOR PROCESSING THIS EXERCISE WITH CLIENT

Children who have difficulty in school frequently have very negative views about school. Unfortunately, where the child has difficulty identifying positive aspects of school, these negative views about school can have an impact on the child's school performance. This assignment is designed to help the child begin to identify things about school that he/she likes.

Review the assignment with the child in the session. Instruct the child that he/she will pretend to be a newspaper reporter who is writing an article about school. The child is to answer the questions about school and provide illustrations where indicated. Review the entire worksheet with the child and parents/guardian. Ask the child to bring the completed worksheet to the next session for review. In the next session, focus on aspects of school that are pleasant for the child and encourage the child to talk about school.

SCHOOL IS OKAY

School, the Place to Be

by reporter _____

_____ School is located in _____ .
(Name of school)   (City)

The principal of this school is _____ .

When we are outside I like to _____ .

My teacher's name is _____ .

My best friend in school is _____ .

My favorite subject is _____ .

Draw a picture of your school.

We have special days in school when we _____

_____ .

Draw a picture of this special day.

I was proud in school when I _____

_____ .

Draw a picture of this day.

HOMEWORK

GOALS OF THE EXERCISE

1. Identify strategies to facilitate homework completion.
2. Develop strategies to help the client complete homework assignments on a regular, consistent basis.
3. Develop a regular homework routine.

ADDITIONAL HOMEWORK THAT MAY BE APPLICABLE TO ACADEMIC ACHIEVEMENT

• ADHD	Establishing Behavioral Plans	Page 70
• Self-Esteem	Goal Setting	Page 313
• School Refusal	Positively School	Page 277
• School Refusal	School in View	Page 281

ADDITIONAL PROBLEMS FOR WHICH THIS EXERCISE MAY BE USEFUL

- ADHD
- Conduct Disorder
- Disruptive Behavior
- Oppositional Defiant Disorder
- Peer Conflict
- School Refusal

SUGGESTIONS FOR PROCESSING THIS EXERCISE WITH CLIENT

A frequent school concern is that the child is not completing homework assignments. This assignment utilizes behavioral strategies to focus on homework completion.

In the therapy session, ask the parents/guardian and child to briefly describe the types of homework the child receives (e.g., math, reading). This review of assignments serves as an assessment of parental involvement as well as the child's ability level in various subject areas. For example, does the child regularly complete the math worksheet but not the reading assignments? Discussion around these issues might begin to identify strengths and weaknesses in specific academic areas. This initial screening might also lead to a referral for an in-depth academic assessment.

In the therapy session, review the goal sheet with the child. Set a goal related to completion of homework assignments. The contract should be reviewed with the child and parents/guardian. Give a copy of the contract to the child. Instruct the child to check off the appropriate box each day when he/she completes the assignment. Review the behavioral chart in the therapy session. Use the therapy session to identify strategies that can facilitate completion of homework assignments.

Review the handout "Tips for Helping Your Child with Homework" with the parents/guardian. This handout encourages parental involvement in the homework process and reviews simple behavioral strategies that can improve homework completion.

HOMEWORK

Homework Contract

I _____ agree to

complete my homework assignments daily.

I will review each day's assignments with

_____

who will sign my homework chart.

Signatures:

_____   _____

_____   _____

Homework

List the assignment in the first column. When each assignment is complete, parent/guardian should review and sign the appropriate column.

Date: _____

Subject Assignment	Monday	Tuesday	Wednesday	Thursday	Friday
Parent's/guardian's signature					

Tips for Helping Your Child with Homework

Families often struggle with issues involving homework. One way to limit this power struggle is to establish a routine for homework completion. Here are some tips for helping your child with his/her homework.

- Set aside a special location for homework. This space should be quiet and have adequate lighting.

- Limit distractions.

- Set aside a specific time each day for homework.

- Review homework with your child.

- Meet with teachers to discuss how your child is doing.

- Remember that homework is your child's responsibility, not yours. Your child will not learn if you complete his/her assignments.

- Help your child organize his/her homework and workbooks.

Section II

ADOPTION

THE STORY OF ADOPTION

GOALS OF THE EXERCISE

1. Tell the story of the adoption through drawings.
2. Express feelings associated with the adoption through art.
3. Begin to develop rapport with the therapist so feelings associated with adoption can be discussed.

ADDITIONAL HOMEWORK THAT MAY BE APPLICABLE TO ADOPTION

ADDITIONAL PROBLEMS FOR WHICH THIS EXERCISE MAY BE USEFUL

- Blended Families
- Divorce

SUGGESTIONS FOR PROCESSING THIS EXERCISE WITH CLIENT

This assignment focuses on children who currently are in the process or who have recently gone through the process of being adopted. The child is asked to draw pictures related to the adoption. These drawings can be used to initiate discussion about feelings such as anxiety, excitement, grief, and loss in the context of a supportive therapeutic relationship. These drawings can be combined and placed in a folder to create an illustrated booklet focusing on changes in the family.

Three drawings are included in this homework assignment. The child will need to draw pictures illustrating the following:

- His/her family prior to adoption
- When he/she found out the adoption was final
- His/her adopted family

These three drawing sessions can be spread over several weeks. Review the instructions with the child in the therapy session. If the child has difficulty reading the worksheets, help him/her with the instructions.

Review each of the drawings with the child. Help the child to verbally express feelings associated with the adoption. Children frequently process feelings through the concrete description of details. When describing how he/she learned about the adoption, the child might focus on very specific details. Do not rush the child. Be sensitive to the child's pace for disclosure.

When all of the drawings are completed, compile them to create a booklet. Assemble these drawings in a colored folder that the child can decorate and that will serve as a cover for this personalized booklet about the adoption. This booklet can be used throughout therapy.

THE STORY OF ADOPTION

Draw a picture of your family before the adoption.

Draw a picture showing how you found out about the adoption.

Draw a picture of your family.

MY ADOPTION

GOALS OF THE EXERCISE

1. Tell the story of the adoption through drawings.
2. Express feelings associated with the adoption through art.
3. Begin to develop rapport with the therapist so feelings associated with the adoption can be discussed.

ADDITIONAL HOMEWORK THAT MAY BE APPLICABLE TO ADOPTION

ADDITIONAL PROBLEMS FOR WHICH THIS EXERCISE MAY BE USEFUL

*   Blended Families
*   Divorce

SUGGESTIONS FOR PROCESSING THIS EXERCISE WITH CLIENT

This assignment focuses on children who have recently learned that they were adopted. The child is asked to draw a picture of how he/she learned about being adopted. This drawing can then be used to initiate discussion about feelings in the context of a supportive therapeutic relationship.

Review the drawing with the child. Help the child to verbally express feelings associated with the adoption. Children frequently process feelings through the concrete description of details. When describing how he/she learned about the adoption, the child might focus on very specific details. Do not rush the child. Be sensitive to the child's pace for disclosure.

MY ADOPTION

Draw a picture of how you found out you were adopted.

YOU ARE THE EXPERT

GOALS OF THE EXERCISE

1. Tell the story of the adoption through drawings.
2. Express feelings associated with the adoption through art.
3. Begin to develop rapport with the therapist so feelings associated with the adoption can be discussed.

ADDITIONAL HOMEWORK THAT MAY BE APPLICABLE TO ADOPTION

ADDITIONAL PROBLEMS FOR WHICH THIS EXERCISE MAY BE USEFUL

- Blended Families
- Divorce

SUGGESTIONS FOR PROCESSING THIS EXERCISE WITH CLIENT

This assignment focuses on children who are in the process or who have recently gone through the process of being adopted. The child is asked to answer questions that might be helpful to other children who are currently in the process of being adopted. The worksheets can then be used to initiate discussion about anxiety, excitement, grief, and loss in the context of a supportive therapeutic relationship.

The child is asked to make a workbook and explain adoption to help children going through a similar process by sharing lessons learned. The child is asked to focus on the adoption in the third person—as an expert who is teaching others. Children often can focus on sensitive issues using this type of strategy. This homework assignment can be started in the therapy session, and the child can provide illustrations for the answers at home. Review the instructions with the child in the therapy session. If the child has difficulty reading the worksheets, help the child with the instructions.

When the child returns the next week, review each of the drawings with him/her. Help the child to verbally express feelings associated with the adoption. Children frequently process feelings through the concrete description of details. When describing how he/she learned about the adoption, the child might focus on very specific details. Do not rush the child. Be sensitive to the child's pace for disclosure.

This assignment can be completed over several weeks, during which the child reviews one or two pages each week. When all of the drawings are completed, compile them to create a booklet. Assemble these drawings in a colored folder that the child can decorate and that will serve as a cover for the booklet. This booklet can be used throughout therapy.

YOU ARE THE EXPERT

There are many children who can learn from your experience with adoption. Answer the questions on each page.

Children who are adopted might feel _____

_____

_____

_____

In each circle draw a picture of a feeling that a child may feel when being adopted.

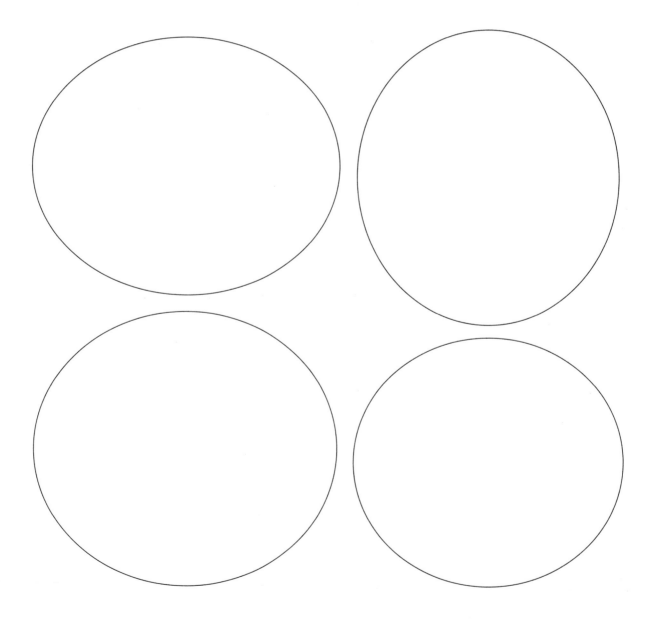

The best thing about adoption is _____ .

Draw a picture of the best thing about adoption.

The worst thing about adoption is _____ .

Draw a picture of the worst thing about adoption.

Tell your story of adoption.

Draw a picture of your adoption.

ANGER MANAGEMENT

ANGER CONTROL

GOALS OF THE EXERCISE

1. Identify the precipitants of feelings of anger.
2. Increase the ability to verbalize feelings of anger.
3. Identify varying levels of anger.
4. Identify two strategies to manage anger more effectively.

ADDITIONAL HOMEWORK THAT MAY BE APPLICABLE TO ANGER MANAGEMENT

• ADHD	Establishing Behavioral Plans	Page 70
• ADHD	Stop and Think	Page 84
• Conduct Disorder	I'm So Frustrated I Could Burst	Page 101
• Disruptive Behavior	Weighing the Options	Page 135
• Disruptive Behavior	Communicating Assertively	Page 139
• Oppositional Defiant Disorder	Improved Communication	Page 200
• Oppositional Defiant Disorder	Another Point of View	Page 207
• Oppositional Defiant Disorder	Conflict Resolution	Page 212

ADDITIONAL PROBLEMS FOR WHICH THIS EXERCISE MAY BE USEFUL

- ADHD
- Conduct Disorder
- Disruptive Behavior
- Fire Setting
- Oppositional Defiant Disorder

SUGGESTIONS FOR PROCESSING THIS EXERCISE WITH CLIENT

This homework assignment is designed for children who have difficulty verbalizing their feelings and managing their anger. For this assignment the child will begin to identify situations in which he/she experiences different emotions. A major goal of this assignment is to help the child identify different feelings and begin to use words to express his/her emotions.

Review the first worksheet in the session and ask the child to identify times when he/she felt afraid, angry, or confused. Read the instructions with the child. The child will most likely require some assistance with these worksheets. Review both worksheets with the child and his/her parents/guardian. For this assignment the child will need to describe or draw a picture of a time when he/she felt various feelings.

When the child brings the worksheet to the next session, have him/her begin to rate the degree of each emotion associated with each situation. Work with the child to help him/her understand the varying degrees of each emotion. Complete the worksheet in the session, asking the child to rate each emotion on the scale.

Use the worksheets to begin to focus on feelings and the precipitants of feelings. The child will begin to become aware of feelings and the frequency with which he/she feels each emotion. This homework assignment can be used to begin discussion about anger and strategies to manage anger.

ANGER CONTROL

Use words or pictures to describe a time when you felt . . .

afraid	angry
confused	embarrassed
excited	frustrated
happy	mad
nervous	sad

Rate how frequently you feel . . .

afraid

1	2	3	4	5
never	not often	sometimes	often	all the time

angry

1	2	3	4	5
never	not often	sometimes	often	all the time

confused

1	2	3	4	5
never	not often	sometimes	often	all the time

disappointed

1	2	3	4	5
never	not often	sometimes	often	all the time

embarrassed

1	2	3	4	5
never	not often	sometimes	often	all the time

excited

1	2	3	4	5
never	not often	sometimes	often	all the time

frustrated

1	2	3	4	5
never	not often	sometimes	often	all the time

guilty

1	2	3	4	5
never	not often	sometimes	often	all the time

happy

1	2	3	4	5
never	not often	sometimes	often	all the time

jealous

1	2	3	4	5
never	not often	sometimes	often	all the time

lonely

1	2	3	4	5
never	not often	sometimes	often	all the time

loved

1	2	3	4	5
never	not often	sometimes	often	all the time

mad

1	2	3	4	5
never	not often	sometimes	often	all the time

nervous

1	2	3	4	5
never	not often	sometimes	often	all the time

proud

1	2	3	4	5
never	not often	sometimes	often	all the time

sad

1	2	3	4	5
never	not often	sometimes	often	all the time

scared

1	2	3	4	5
never	not often	sometimes	often	all the time

worried

1	2	3	4	5
never	not often	sometimes	often	all the time

ANGER MANAGEMENT

GOALS OF THE EXERCISE

1. Identify strategies for coping with anger.
2. Identify two strategies to manage anger more effectively.
3. Develop problem-solving skills.

ADDITIONAL HOMEWORK THAT MAY BE APPLICABLE TO ANGER MANAGEMENT

- ADHD   Establishing Behavioral Plans   Page 70
- ADHD   Stop and Think   Page 84
- Conduct Disorder   I'm So Frustrated I Could Burst   Page 101
- Disruptive Behavior   Weighing the Options   Page 135
- Disruptive Behavior   Communicating Assertively   Page 139
- Oppositional Defiant Disorder   Improved Communication   Page 200
- Oppositional Defiant Disorder   Another Point of View   Page 207
- Oppositional Defiant Disorder   Conflict Resolution   Page 212

ADDITIONAL PROBLEMS FOR WHICH THIS EXERCISE MAY BE USEFUL

- ADHD
- Conduct Disorder
- Disruptive Behavior
- Fire Setting
- Oppositional Defiant Disorder

SUGGESTIONS FOR PROCESSING THIS EXERCISE WITH CLIENT

This homework assignment is designed for children who have difficulty managing their anger. The first step in developing anger management skills involves understanding the precipitants of anger and anger outbursts. Once the precipitants are identified, therapy can focus on anger management strategies.

For this assignment the child will begin to identify situations that make him/her angry. Identification of these situations is critical in the development of anger management skills, for the child will begin to understand what situations are particularly difficult for him/her.

The first worksheet instructs the child to draw pictures of or describe situations in which he/she becomes angry. The second worksheet encourages the child to identify strategies for managing anger. Read the instructions with the child. The child will most likely require some assistance with these worksheets. Review both worksheets with the child and his/her parents/guardian.

When the child brings the worksheet to the next session, have him/her begin to rate the degree of anger associated with each situation. Work with the child to help him/her understand varying degrees of anger.

Also, begin a discussion about the strategies that the child typically uses to manage his/her anger. The therapy session can be used to help the child understand the potential consequences of each reaction and to rate the effectiveness of these strategies. In this session, the therapist can begin to instruct the child about alternative strategies that the child has not used in the past. These include counting to 10 to cool down, exercising, taking a walk, and talking to someone. While discussing strategies, focus on the effectiveness of each strategy in various situations.

ANGER MANAGEMENT

Things That Make Me Angry

In each star, draw a picture of a time when you were angry.

What Can I Do When I Get Angry?

List 10 things you can do when you get angry:

1. _____

2. _____

3. _____

4. _____

5. _____

6. _____

7. _____

8. _____

9. _____

10. _____

SOLVING A PROBLEM

GOALS OF THE EXERCISE

1. Identify the precipitants of feelings of anger.
2. Increase the ability to verbalize feelings of anger.
3. Identify strategies for coping with anger.
4. Identify varying levels of anger.
5. Identify two strategies to manage anger more effectively.

ADDITIONAL HOMEWORK THAT MAY BE APPLICABLE TO ANGER MANAGEMENT

ADDITIONAL PROBLEMS FOR WHICH THIS EXERCISE MAY BE USEFUL

- ADHD
- Conduct Disorder
- Disruptive Behavior
- Fire Setting
- Oppositional Defiant Disorder
- Peer Conflict

SUGGESTIONS FOR PROCESSING THIS EXERCISE WITH CLIENT

This homework assignment is designed for children who have difficulty managing their anger.

In previous homework assignments the child has identified situations that make him/her angry. Identification of these situations is critical in the development of anger management skills, for the child begins to understand what situations are particularly difficult for him/her. This homework assignment focuses on anger management strategies.

Read the instructions with the child. The child will most likely require some assistance with these worksheets. Review both worksheets with the child and his/her parents/guardian.

The therapy session can be used to help the child understand the potential consequences of each reaction and to rate the effectiveness of each of these strategies. In this session, the therapist can also begin to instruct the child about alternative strategies that the child has not used in the past. These include counting to 10 to cool down, exercising, taking a walk, and talking to someone. While discussing strategies, focus on the utility of each strategy in various situations.

Describe the problem-solving worksheet in detail in the session. Be certain to review one or two examples in the session. For the homework assignment, complete the top portion of the worksheet, using a situation that is difficult for the child (one in which the child frequently has difficulty managing his/her anger). Instruct the child to list five alternatives and the consequences of each alternative. Help the child problem-solve by reviewing the alternatives and consequences to determine the best choice.

SOLVING A PROBLEM

When I become angry, I usually

_____

which results in

_____

Instead, when I become angry I can cool down by:

counting to 10

exercising

taking a walk

talking to someone

playing sports

going to my room

_____

_____

_____

_____

_____

Problem Solving

Problem

Alternatives

1.   2.   3.   4.   5.

Consequences of each alternative

1.   2.   3.   4.   5.

What is the best choice?

Section IV

ANXIETY

COPING WITH ANXIETY

GOALS OF THE EXERCISE

1. Identify the precipitants of feelings of anxiety.
2. Increase the ability to verbalize feelings of anxiety.
3. Identify strategies for coping with anxiety.
4. Identify varying levels of anxiety.
5. Identify a visual image of a place where the child feels relaxed. (This image can be used in later therapy sessions to complete visualization relaxation exercises.)

ADDITIONAL HOMEWORK THAT MAY BE APPLICABLE TO ANXIETY

• Depression	Communicating Feelings	Page 116
• Depression	Rewriting Cognitive Distortions	Page 130
• Self-Esteem	Self-Improvement	Page 296
• Separation Anxiety	I Can Do It Myself	Page 318
• Separation Anxiety	Fun with Friends	Page 322
• Separation Anxiety	Separation Feelings	Page 325
• Separation Anxiety	Steps to Independence	Page 328
• Specific Phobia	Overcoming Fears	Page 368

ADDITIONAL PROBLEMS FOR WHICH THIS EXERCISE MAY BE USEFUL

- Depression
- Self-Esteem
- Separation Anxiety
- Social Phobia
- Specific Phobia

SUGGESTIONS FOR PROCESSING THIS EXERCISE WITH CLIENT

Young children frequently feel nervous or anxious and have difficulty verbalizing these feelings. Anxiety can be related to concerns about family, school, or peers, or to pressures associated with performance. Children also have difficulty understanding that anxiety has varying degrees. This assignment will help the child understand that different situations are associated with varying levels of anxiety.

This assignment can be completed over multiple weeks. The first step in this assignment is to identify a specific time when the child felt nervous or anxious and draw a picture representing this time. This drawing will allow the child to begin the discussion about anxiety. The first drawing can be completed in the therapy session, with the follow-up worksheets being completed at home. This first drawing sets the framework for the other worksheets, which look at precipitants of anxiety and levels of anxiety.

After the child has identified and concretely described one situation in which he/she has felt anxious, the next step is to help the child recognize the links between worrying and anxiety. The child is asked to identify situations in which he/she worries. The directions for this assignment are simple; however, they should be clearly reviewed in the therapy session. Read the directions with the child in the therapy session. Instruct the child to draw pictures in each of the circles showing situations in which he/she worries or gets nervous.

The next step in this assignment involves having the child rate feelings of anxiety from 0 to 5. The child reads a short passage about anxiety and uses the worksheet to rate the levels of anxiety described. This assignment requires the child to identify various levels of anxiety. When discussing this worksheet, help the child to identify situations in which he/she has felt anxiety at the various levels.

The final step in this assignment is to create a visual image of a place where the child feels calm and relaxed. This image can be used in future therapy sessions when relaxation techniques are taught.

COPING WITH ANXIETY

Think about a time when you were nervous. Draw a picture showing a time when you recently felt nervous.

Do you ever worry about things? In the circles draw pictures of the things about which you worry or situations that make you feel nervous.

Johnny sometimes gets very nervous. He has noticed that some situations make him extremely nervous, others a little nervous, and others a tiny bit nervous.

When Johnny <u>goes to bed</u> he is <u>not nervous at all</u>.

When Johnny has a <u>test</u> he is <u>extremely nervous</u>.

When Johnny <u>talks in front</u> of his class he is a <u>little nervous</u>.

When Johnny <u>meets a new friend</u> he is a <u>tiny bit nervous</u>.

When Johnny recites a <u>poem in front of the whole school</u> he is <u>very nervous</u>.

When Johnny has a <u>quiz</u> he is <u>moderately nervous</u>.

Using the scale on this page, help Johnny rate the situations from 0 to 5. Write the underlined words in the correct spaces to show how nervous Johnny gets with each situation.

extremely nervous	5	_____
very nervous	4	_____
moderately (medium) nervous	3	_____
a little nervous	2	_____
a tiny bit nervous	1	_____
not nervous at all	0	_____

Think of a calm and peaceful place. This place can be someplace that you visited or a place you saw on TV or read about in a book. Think about this place for a few minutes. Imagine all of the details about this special place. Draw a picture of this place where you have felt calm and peaceful.

UNREALISTIC FEARS

GOALS OF THE EXERCISE

1. Identify cognitive messages that mediate anxiety.
2. Learn to verbalize cognitive messages that mediate anxiety.
3. Begin to understand the relationship between cognitive messages and feelings of anxiety.

ADDITIONAL HOMEWORK THAT MAY BE APPLICABLE TO ANXIETY

ADDITIONAL PROBLEMS FOR WHICH THIS EXERCISE MAY BE USEFUL

- Depression
- Self-Esteem
- Separation Anxiety
- Social Phobia
- Specific Phobia

SUGGESTIONS FOR PROCESSING THIS EXERCISE WITH CLIENT

Anxiety for young children as well as for adults is frequently not based on actual experiences. Instead, fears may be exaggerated and at times completely unrealistic. A small worry about a situation can snowball into excessive anxiety or great fear. Helping children understand the link between cognitive messages and feelings of anxiety can be of lifelong benefit.

The first section of this assignment should be completed with parents/guardian. The child is asked to read a short story and identify unrealistic fears. The child will need much assistance to recognize unrealistic or distorted cognitions. Next, the child is asked to list five things about which he/she worries. In the therapy session the child will focus on whether these worries are realistic or not. Instruct the child and parents/guardian that the next part of the worksheet will be completed in the therapy session. The review of cognitive distortions should be completed with parents/guardian because it can be helpful for those who might reinforce distorted, anxiety-provoking cognitions.

UNREALISTIC FEARS

Sometimes we worry about things that will never happen. For example, Tommy worried that his friends would tease him about his haircut. His friends never teased him. In fact, one girl even told him he looked good.

He used a lot of energy worrying about the teasing that never happened. Other times we worry about things and exaggerate what we think might happen. For example, Tommy worried about failing a test and thought that if he failed the test his sister would tease him.

In school, Tommy did not fail—he got a C. Later he thought that if he hadn't worried, he might have done even better.

What was Tommy worrying about?

1.

2.

Did his fear that his friends would tease him come true?

Did his fear that his sister would tease him come true?

Sometimes I worry that . . .

1. _____

_____

_____

2. _____

_____

_____

3. _____

_____

_____

4. _____

_____

_____

5. _____

_____

_____

In-session review of the evidence for these fears:

1. _____

_____

_____

2. _____

_____

_____

3. _____

_____

_____

4. _____

_____

_____

5. _____

_____

_____

MANAGING ANXIETY

GOALS OF THE EXERCISE

1. Identify fears, worries, and anxiety.
2. Increase the ability to verbalize feelings of anxiety.
3. Identify varying levels of anxiety.
4. Identify strategies for managing anxiety.

ADDITIONAL HOMEWORK THAT MAY BE APPLICABLE TO ANXIETY

ADDITIONAL PROBLEMS FOR WHICH THIS EXERCISE MAY BE USEFUL

- Depression
- Self-Esteem
- Separation Anxiety
- Social Phobia
- Specific Phobia

SUGGESTIONS FOR PROCESSING THIS EXERCISE WITH CLIENT

For this homework assignment the child will begin to identify the precipitants of anxiety and strategies to manage anxiety more effectively. In the therapy session, help the child verbalize several worries and situations in which he/she gets nervous. As homework, the child will draw a picture for each worksheet. On the first sheet the child is asked to draw a picture of something about which he/she worries. The second worksheet requests that the child identify situations in which he/she gets nervous. Instruct the child to complete only the top section of both pages. Inform the child that the next therapy session will focus on strategies to manage anxiety. Therefore, during the week the child can consult with parents/guardian about strategies.

After the child has identified and concretely described one situation in which he/she has felt anxious, the next step is to help the child recognize the links between worrying and anxiety. In the session, help the child develop new strategies for managing anxiety (e.g., relaxation strategies). The child will draw a picture illustrating the strategy that he/she believes will be most successful in managing anxiety.

MANAGING ANXIETY

I worry about (draw a picture of something that you worry about):

```



```

(To be completed in therapy session)

What can I do when I worry?

```



```

I get nervous when (draw a picture of a situation that makes you nervous):

(To be completed in therapy session)

What can I do when I get nervous?

STRESS MANAGEMENT

GOALS OF THE EXERCISE

1. Identify stress management techniques.
2. Practice stress management techniques.
3. Identify stressors.
4. Identify stress level.

ADDITIONAL HOMEWORK THAT MAY BE APPLICABLE TO ANXIETY

• Depression	Communicating Feelings	Page 116
• Depression	Rewriting Cognitive Distortions	Page 130
• Self-Esteem	Self-Improvement	Page 296
• Separation Anxiety	I Can Do It Myself	Page 318
• Separation Anxiety	Fun with Friends	Page 322
• Separation Anxiety	Separation Feelings	Page 325
• Separation Anxiety	Steps to Independence	Page 328
• Specific Phobia	Overcoming Fears	Page 368

ADDITIONAL PROBLEMS FOR WHICH THIS EXERCISE MAY BE USEFUL

- Depression
- Self-Esteem
- Separation Anxiety
- Social Phobia
- Specific Phobia

SUGGESTIONS FOR PROCESSING THIS EXERCISE WITH CLIENT

This homework assignment can be used with any child who is experiencing stressors. This homework assignment is to be completed over multiple weeks.

This assignment includes the following activities:

- Identifying physical symptoms of stress
- Identifying stress levels associated with specific situations
- Identifying daily stress level

Read the instructions for each worksheet to the child in the session. The child will complete the assignment at home and review the worksheet in the next session. The second worksheet can be completed in the session to help the child understand varying levels of stress and to introduce the third worksheet, which asks the child to rate stress levels.

The third worksheet can be used as a weekly monitor of stress levels and to measure the effectiveness of the stress management techniques over time. This monitor of stress levels can be used to document a decrease in stress level over time and to identify patterns of stressors.

STRESS MANAGEMENT

Our bodies react to stress in different ways. Draw a picture of yourself when you are under stress.

Circle the ways that you typically react to stress:

feel irritated   have headache   feel sweaty

heart races   feel nervous   palms get sweaty   feel very cold

Identifying when we are under stress is the first step to coping with it. Rate from 1 to 8 how stressful these situations would be for you (1 = not stressful; 8 = very stressful).

Failing a test	1 2 3 4 5 6 7 8
Having a fight with a friend	1 2 3 4 5 6 7 8
Parents fighting	1 2 3 4 5 6 7 8
Moving to a new home	1 2 3 4 5 6 7 8
Talking in front of your class	1 2 3 4 5 6 7 8
Difficult homework assignment	1 2 3 4 5 6 7 8
Friend pressuring you to do something you don't want to do	1 2 3 4 5 6 7 8
Close friend moves far away	1 2 3 4 5 6 7 8
Getting teased	1 2 3 4 5 6 7 8
Being embarrassed in front of your class	1 2 3 4 5 6 7 8
Forgetting your homework	1 2 3 4 5 6 7 8
Going to a party where you know few people	1 2 3 4 5 6 7 8
Having an argument with your parents/guardian	1 2 3 4 5 6 7 8

Rate your level of stress this week.

Monday	1	2	3	4	5	6	7	8
	low stress							high stress
Tuesday	1	2	3	4	5	6	7	8
	low stress							high stress
Wednesday	1	2	3	4	5	6	7	8
	low stress							high stress
Thursday	1	2	3	4	5	6	7	8
	low stress							high stress
Friday	1	2	3	4	5	6	7	8
	low stress							high stress
Saturday	1	2	3	4	5	6	7	8
	low stress							high stress
Sunday	1	2	3	4	5	6	7	8
	low stress							high stress

RELAXATION

GOALS OF THE EXERCISE

1. Identify strategies to manage stress.
2. Identify a visual image of a place where the child feels relaxed.
3. Identify an individual with whom the child can talk when he/she feels stressed.

ADDITIONAL HOMEWORK THAT MAY BE APPLICABLE TO ANXIETY

ADDITIONAL PROBLEMS FOR WHICH THIS EXERCISE MAY BE USEFUL

- Depression
- Self-Esteem
- Separation Anxiety
- Social Phobia
- Specific Phobia

SUGGESTIONS FOR PROCESSING THIS EXERCISE WITH CLIENT

This homework assignment is designed for children who have difficulty with anxiety. Unlike the other assignments in this section, it focuses exclusively on relaxation strategies. For this assignment the child is asked to visualize and draw pictures of relaxing situations.

The first activity in this assignment instructs the child to imagine himself/herself using a variety of strategies to manage anxiety. Review the list of strategies in the session and instruct the child to complete the four drawings.

The last three activities can be completed over several weeks. The child will draw three pictures related to stress management. When the child completes the drawings, they can be compiled into a booklet.

RELAXATION

There are many things you can do to relieve stress. Draw pictures of yourself using the following strategies to cope with a stressful situation.

Exercising

Relaxing

Doing something fun

Talking to someone

Draw a special place that helps you feel calm and relaxed.

Draw a picture of a special activity that helps you feel calm and relaxed.

Draw a picture of someone that you can talk to when you are feeling stressed.

Section V

ATTENTION-DEFICIT/HYPERACTIVITY DISORDER

ESTABLISHING BEHAVIORAL PLANS

GOALS OF THE EXERCISE

1. Educate the parents/guardian about behavioral strategies that can be used to manage behavior more effectively.
2. Decrease behavioral difficulties.
3. Develop an effective behavioral plan.

ADDITIONAL HOMEWORK THAT MAY BE APPLICABLE TO ATTENTION-DEFICIT/HYPERACTIVITY DISORDER

• Anger Management	Anger Control	Page 31
• Anger Management	Anger Management	Page 36
• Anger Management	Solving a Problem	Page 40
• Conduct Disorder	I'm So Frustrated I Could Burst	Page 101
• Disruptive Behavior	Weighing the Options	Page 135
• Oppositional Defiant Disorder	Improved Communication	Page 200
• Oppositional Defiant Disorder	Conflict Resolution	Page 212

ADDITIONAL PROBLEMS FOR WHICH THIS EXERCISE MAY BE USEFUL

- Anger Management
- Conduct Disorder
- Disruptive Behavior
- Enuresis
- Oppositional Defiant Disorder

SUGGESTIONS FOR PROCESSING THIS EXERCISE WITH CLIENT

Many children with ADHD have difficulty maintaining appropriate behavior. This homework assignment will teach parents/guardian basic strategies for developing an effective behavioral plan.

This behavioral plan can be used by teachers or parents/guardian. Once the parents/guardian have effectively used the behavior chart at home, the plan can be slightly modified for school behavior. Give the parents/guardian the overview sheet that describes how to establish a behavioral plan.

This assignment has three parts. In the first week, the parents/guardian gather information about the child's behavior; describe alternative, more appropriate behaviors; and identify potential rewards. For the first week, instruct the parents/guardian to observe a specific problematic behavior—for example, fighting with a sibling, not completing homework, or whining. Review the instructions with the parents/guardian. Have them monitor the child's behavior and note the date, time, precipitants, and special circumstances associated with each behavior. For the second sheet, also completed in the first week, the parents/guardian must describe alternative behaviors that would be more appropriate and document times when the child has exhibited these behaviors. Finally, the parents/guardian will list possible rewards for the child.

After the parents/guardian have compiled this information, develop the behavioral plan with the parents/guardian and child during the therapy session. Writing a behavioral plan can be difficult, so it is important to complete this task in the therapy session.

Based on the observations of the child's behavior, write a goal that is realistic for the week. Behavioral plans should focus on increasing positive and appropriate behaviors. Use the alternative appropriate behaviors listed by the parents/guardian to write the behavioral plan. Be certain to focus on the positive when writing the behavioral plan.

Focus on one target goal. Describe the behavior that you want to encourage. For example:

Billy will put his dinner plate in the sink after dinner.
Jane will complete her homework each night.
Bobby will tell his mother when his younger sister teases him.

Clearly review the behavior with the child. It is helpful to role-play the behavior in the therapy session. Be very specific about the behavior that you want to increase (if possible, note the number of times each day and the specific location). Repeat the goal several times and be certain that the child understands the assignment.

Write out the goal on the behavioral plan. Inform the parents/guardian that each time the child exhibits the appropriate behavior, he/she should place a star on the chart. Determine the reward and number of times that the behavior should be present to earn the reward. Review the contract with the child and parents/guardian. Have both child and parents/guardian sign the behavioral plan.

The third part of this assignment involves the actual implementation of the behavioral plan. If the plan is thoroughly reviewed in the session and all parties (parents/guardian, child, and therapist) understand the plan, it will be more effective. Each week the behavioral plan should be reviewed and modified based on the child's behavior. As the child's behavior begins to change, make the reward less frequent. Remember that all successful behavioral plans start with small changes.

ESTABLISHING BEHAVIORAL PLANS

The goal of this assignment is to develop an effective behavior management chart to help your child manage problematic behaviors.

1.   The first step in any behavioral plan is to identify the frequency and the pattern of problematic behaviors. This step involves observing your child's behavior and looking specifically for patterns. It is important to note any discrepancies or patterns in the behavior. For example, does your child have difficulty after meals, or with certain activities or certain friends? It is critical for you to have a good understanding of the behavior before we start to make the behavioral plan. The behavioral plan must be realistic—so you must observe your child to determine the baseline for this behavior.

     To determine a baseline, you will record incidents of this behavior throughout the week. You will also note changes in this behavior. Once you have identified the baseline of behavior, we will use this information to develop a realistic behavioral plan.

2.   During this week also look for times when your child responds to similar situations with more appropriate behaviors. List more appropriate behavioral alternatives on the second worksheet. When we create the behavioral plan we will want your child to increase these alternative, more appropriate behaviors.

3.   The final step of this week's assignment is for you to compile a list of possible rewards for your child. You will use this list to establish your reward system.

The goal of a behavioral plan is to increase appropriate behavior and decrease problematic behavior. This can be done in one of two ways: (1) rewarding appropriate behavior and ignoring problematic behavior or (2) setting consequences for problematic behavior. Research indicates that reward is always more effective.

Monitoring Sheet for Behaviors

On this sheet, record the occurrence of this behavior: _____ . Be sure to note what happened prior to the behavior and any special circumstances.

Date/day	Time	Precipitants	Special Circumstances

Describe more appropriate behaviors that your child can use rather than the problematic behavior. Also, note times when your child has exhibited more appropriate behaviors.

_____

_____

_____

_____

_____

_____

_____

List 10 possible rewards that can be used for your child. Be certain to include activities that your child likes. There are many types of rewards, including material items, activities, praise, and special treats.

1. _____

2. _____

3. _____

4. _____

5. _____

6. _____

7. _____

8. _____

9. _____

10. _____

Behavior I want to change: _____

Goal for this week: _____

Reward: _____

Signatures: _____
        (parent/guardian)   (child)   (therapist)

Instructions: Each time _____ exhibits the following behavior _____ place a star on the chart for the appropriate day.

Sunday
_____

Monday
_____

Tuesday
_____

Wednesday
_____

Thursday
_____

Friday
_____

Saturday
_____

DAILY ROUTINE

GOALS OF THE EXERCISE

1. Help parents/guardian develop a daily routine for children.
2. Educate parents/guardian about behavioral strategies that can be used to manage behavior more effectively.
3. Decrease behavior difficulties.

ADDITIONAL HOMEWORK THAT MAY BE APPLICABLE TO ATTENTION-DEFICIT/HYPERACTIVITY DISORDER

• Anger Management	Anger Control	Page 31
• Anger Management	Anger Management	Page 36
• Anger Management	Solving a Problem	Page 40
• Conduct Disorder	I'm So Frustrated I Could Burst	Page 101
• Disruptive Behavior	Weighing the Options	Page 135
• Oppositional Defiant Disorder	Improved Communication	Page 200
• Oppositional Defiant Disorder	Conflict Resolution	Page 212

ADDITIONAL PROBLEMS FOR WHICH THIS EXERCISE MAY BE USEFUL

• Anger Management
• Conduct Disorder
• Enuresis
• Mental Retardation
• Oppositional Defiant Disorder

SUGGESTIONS FOR PROCESSING THIS EXERCISE WITH CLIENT

This homework assignment is designed specifically for the parents/guardian. The hand-out "Establishing a Routine" should be reviewed with the parents/guardian in the session. Discuss the importance of structure and family routines. For the assignment, the parents/guardian should map out the child's routine for the week and bring the log sheet to the next therapy session for review. In the session, identify areas where routines can be improved. This routine should include regular bedtimes, meals, and activities. There are many behavioral difficulties that can be attributed to lack of sleep or lack of structure. The establishment of regular routines can result in dramatic behavioral improvements.

Obviously, there will be variations in this schedule under certain circumstances. The goal of this exercise is to develop a regular routine and structure for the child and family.

DAILY ROUTINE

Establishing a Routine

Children respond well to schedules and routines. Therefore, it is important to establish a daily routine for your child. It is particularly helpful to establish routines for meals, morning, and bedtime.

- A bedtime routine might include brushing teeth, washing up, putting on pajamas, reading a book, and lights out. The exact details of the routine are not important; the consistency of this routine is the issue.
- Similarly, in the morning establish routines for brushing teeth, getting dressed, and eating breakfast.
- Establish a regular weekly schedule for your child and family.
- Set aside specific family time for games and trips.
- Be certain to have time when your child can get exercise and burn off energy.
- Plan special days and activities. Special days do not require extra money. For example, designate one evening a week as pizza day, plan special breakfast morning, or schedule taco night, when everyone helps with the preparation.
- Use chores as a way to establish special time with your children. Schedule one-on-one time with a child, during which you can complete household chores (e.g., folding laundry and telling stories from the day).
- Limit television time. Be aware of the television programs your child is watching.
- Use the time during which you are watching television programs to build relationships with your children. Often television programs can open discussion of critical issues. Encourage your child to discuss these issues and ask questions he/she may have.

Use this sheet to document your child's daily routine (include wakeup time and bedtime routine). These routines will vary with the age of the child.

Time	Sunday	Monday	Tuesday	Wednesday	Thursday	Friday	Saturday
6:00 a.m.							
7:00							
8:00							
9:00							
10:00							
11:00							
12:00							
1:00							
2:00							
3:00							
4:00							
5:00							
6:00							
7:00							
8:00							
9:00 p.m.							

PARENTING TIPS

GOALS OF THE EXERCISE

1. Educate the parents/guardian about behavioral strategies that can be used to manage behavior more effectively.
2. Decrease behavioral difficulties.

ADDITIONAL HOMEWORK THAT MAY BE APPLICABLE TO ATTENTION-DEFICIT/HYPERACTIVITY DISORDER

• Anger Management	Anger Control	Page 31
• Anger Management	Anger Management	Page 36
• Anger Management	Solving a Problem	Page 40
• Conduct Disorder	I'm So Frustrated I Could Burst	Page 101
• Disruptive Behavior	Weighing the Options	Page 135
• Oppositional Defiant Disorder	Improved Communication	Page 200
• Oppositional Defiant Disorder	Conflict Resolution	Page 212

ADDITIONAL PROBLEMS FOR WHICH THIS EXERCISE MAY BE USEFUL

*   Anger Management
*   Conduct Disorder
*   Enuresis
*   Oppositional Defiant Disorder

SUGGESTIONS FOR PROCESSING THIS EXERCISE WITH CLIENT

This homework assignment is designed specifically for parents/guardian. Review the handouts in the therapy session with the parents/guardian. In the session, focus on behavioral issues that are problematic, and practice behavioral management strategies within the therapy session. These handouts are best used in conjunction with behavioral charts.

Review the two handouts with the parents/guardian and determine the behavioral strategy that will be implemented this week. Have the parents/guardian record the success in changing their behavioral strategies. Instruct the parents/guardian to use the log sheet to record the success of the strategies. In the therapy session, encourage the parents/guardian to identify one behavior that can be targeted and the strategies to be used.

PARENTING TIPS

Tips for Setting Rules

- Explain rules in clear and simple terms. Use words that your child can understand.
- Give only one instruction at a time.
- Have your child repeat your instructions.
- Speak calmly. Do not get angry when describing a rule.
- Do not make the rules too complicated. Focus only on relevant information.
- Do not attack your child's self-esteem.
- Rules should be reasonable and age appropriate.
- Set logical consequences for each rule.
- Be consistent.
- When a rule is broken, give your child a reminder of the rule and the consequences.
- Often children behave inappropriately or act out when they cannot cope with their feelings. It is important to help children express their feelings. Sometimes instead of making rules it is more important to understand the child's feelings and behavior.
- Reinforce positive behavior.
- Ignore inappropriate behavior that can be ignored.
- Do not make threats or promises that you will not or cannot keep.

Setting Limits

When communicating with your child:

- Be certain that there are no distractions.
- Get your child's attention.
- Make one request at a time.
- Repeat instructions.

When setting limits, set logical consequences. For example, if your child is 10 minutes late returning home from a friend's house, he/she must come home 10 minutes early the next day.

Helping Your Child Develop Problem-Solving Skills

Sometimes it is critical for you, as the parent, to make the decisions for your child. There are, however, other situations in which your child can be coached by you to solve a problem and identify a solution.

The first step in using this strategy is your analysis of whether this specific problem can be used to teach problem-solving skills.

You are the best judge of whether your child has the ability to solve a specific problem. Be sure that your expectations are age appropriate.

Once you have decided that your child can solve the problem, you can begin to use the following steps to help him/her solve the problem.

1. Have your child describe the problem in simple terms.

2. Help your child use words to describe how he/she feels about the problem.

3. Have your child list all the possible solutions to the problem without evaluating any of the alternatives.

4. Help your child identify the consequences of each of the these alternatives.

5. Choose the best solution.

Log Sheet

Problem Behavior	Strategy Used	Effectiveness

STOP AND THINK

GOALS OF THE EXERCISE

1. Decrease behavioral difficulties.
2. Improve problem-solving skills.
3. Reduce impulsive behavior.

ADDITIONAL HOMEWORK THAT MAY BE APPLICABLE TO ATTENTION-DEFICIT/HYPERACTIVITY DISORDER

ADDITIONAL PROBLEMS FOR WHICH THIS EXERCISE MAY BE USEFUL

*   Anger Management
*   Conduct Disorder
*   Enuresis
*   Oppositional Defiant Disorder

SUGGESTIONS FOR PROCESSING THIS EXERCISE WITH CLIENT

This assignment is designed for children who frequently act impulsively and have poor problem-solving skills. The goal of this assignment is to help the client consider alternatives and develop problem-solving skills.

The first step in this assignment requires the child to answer questions about times when his/her behavior was out of control. This assignment will help the child begin to recognize precipitants of disruptive behavior. As part of this assignment the child will also begin to recognize consequences of impulsive behavior.

The second part of this assignment can be completed in the therapy session. Using the previous worksheets, identify one problem on which to focus in the session. The child will begin to identify alternatives and consequences of each alternative, and develop problem-solving skills.

When completing the problem-solving worksheet, write the problem in the space provided at the top of the page. Encourage the child to identify all possible alternatives (both positive and negative). The consequences of each alternative are listed on the lines. Then the child will need to choose the best solution to the problem.

STOP AND THINK

Think of one time when you lost control.

What happened before you lost control?

_____

_____

_____

What happened that you lost control?

_____

_____

How did you react? What did you do?

_____

_____

How did your family react?

_____

_____

How did your friends react?

_____

_____

How did you feel later that day?

_____

_____

What else could you have done?

_____

_____

How did you regain control?

_____

_____

Problem:

_____

_____

_____

_____

Alternatives   **Consequences of each alternative**

1._____ → 1._____

2._____ → 2._____

3._____ → 3._____

4._____ → 4._____

5._____ → 5._____

6._____ → 6._____

7._____ → 7._____

What is the best choice?

_____

_____

_____

_____

Section VI

BLENDED FAMILIES

FAMILY STORY

GOALS OF THE EXERCISE

1. Verbalize feelings associated with changes in the family.
2. Improve communication between family members.

ADDITIONAL HOMEWORK THAT MAY BE APPLICABLE TO BLENDED FAMILIES

• Divorce	Coping with Divorce	Page 145
• Divorce	Since the Divorce	Page 149
• Self-Esteem	Bill of Rights	Page 305
• Self-Esteem	Wishes	Page 308
• Self-Esteem	Goal Setting	Page 313

ADDITIONAL PROBLEMS FOR WHICH THIS EXERCISE MAY BE USEFUL

- Adoption
- Divorce
- Grief/Loss

SUGGESTIONS FOR PROCESSING THIS EXERCISE WITH CLIENT

This homework assignment is designed for the entire family. Review the instructions for the assignment with the child and the family. The family will write the story about how they became a family. The parents/guardian will fill in the blanks and answer questions about how they united. The child(ren) will illustrate the story. The worksheets will be combined to create a booklet about the family. This family project can be completed over several weeks. The booklet should be reviewed in a family session, during which the family can begin to process feelings associated with this assignment.

FAMILY STORY

THE

_____

(name)

FAMILY

STORY

The members of our family are _____

_____

Draw a picture of your family.

We live at _____

(address)

Draw a picture of your home.

We became a family when _____

_____

_____

_____

_____

Draw a picture of your family doing something together.

Our happiest memory is _____

_____

_____

_____

_____

Draw a picture of your happiest memory.

FAMILY CREST

GOALS OF THE EXERCISE

1. Verbalize feelings associated with changes in the family.
2. Improve communication between family members.

ADDITIONAL HOMEWORK THAT MAY BE APPLICABLE TO BLENDED FAMILIES

ADDITIONAL PROBLEMS FOR WHICH THIS EXERCISE MAY BE USEFUL

- Adoption
- Divorce
- Grief/Loss

SUGGESTIONS FOR PROCESSING THIS EXERCISE WITH CLIENT

This homework assignment is designed for the entire family. Review the instructions with the entire family. Instruct the parents/guardian and child(ren) to create a family crest. Each family member must be present during the creation of the crest. A secretary/recorder must be elected, who will briefly describe the process of creating the crest. The family must unanimously describe how the crest will be designed and what feature(s) will be included on the crest. In the next session, the family will present the crest and describe the process for completing the assignment. This assignment encourages the family to work together to create a family crest.

FAMILY CREST

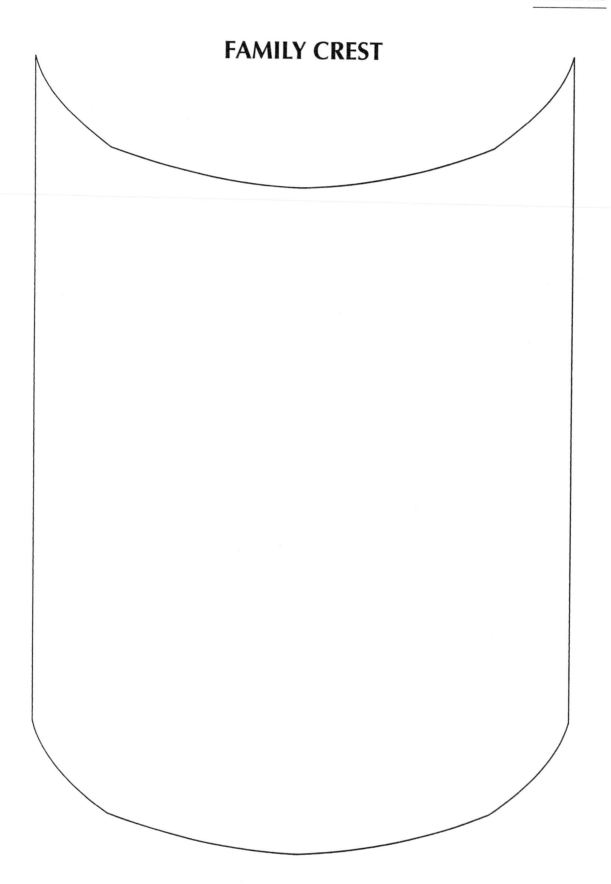

Recorder Notes

How did your family create your family crest?

FAMILY INTERVIEW

GOALS OF THE EXERCISE

1. Verbalize feelings associated with changes in the family.
2. Improve communication between family members.

ADDITIONAL HOMEWORK THAT MAY BE APPLICABLE TO BLENDED FAMILIES

• Divorce	Coping with Divorce	Page 145
• Divorce	Since the Divorce	Page 149
• Self-Esteem	Bill of Rights	Page 305
• Self-Esteem	Wishes	Page 308
• Self-Esteem	Goal Setting	Page 313

ADDITIONAL PROBLEMS FOR WHICH THIS EXERCISE MAY BE USEFUL

- Adoption
- Divorce
- Grief/Loss

SUGGESTIONS FOR PROCESSING THIS EXERCISE WITH CLIENT

This homework assignment encourages communication between family members. The assignment encourages the child to gather information about each family member. More than one child can be assigned to interview family members. In the therapy session, assign the reporter (the child) and the recorder (a parent or an older child). The reporter will interview each family member with the assistance of the recorder. The reporter will ask every question, and the recorder will document all responses. Several copies of the interview sheet may be used to gather information about each family member. The entire family must attend the next therapy session, where the reporter and the recorder will present the information gathered in the interviews.

The format for the presentation of the information can be modified slightly in the therapy session, whereby the reporter and recorder serve as game show hosts. The remaining family members must guess the answers given by each family member.

FAMILY INTERVIEW

Name: _____

1. What is your favorite color?

2. What is your favorite food?

3. What is your favorite song?

4. What was your best birthday celebration?

5. What was your most embarrassing moment?

6. If you had three wishes, for what would you wish?

7. What is your favorite book?

8. What is your favorite television show?

Section VII

CONDUCT DISORDER

I'M SO FRUSTRATED I COULD BURST

GOALS OF THE EXERCISE

1. Become aware of and verbalize feelings.
2. Identify strategies to manage frustration more effectively.
3. Become aware of the association between feelings and reactive behavior.
4. Recognize that difficulties can arise when the severity of the response does not match the situation.

ADDITIONAL HOMEWORK THAT MAY BE APPLICABLE TO CONDUCT DISORDER

• Anger Management	Anger Control	Page 31
• Anger Management	Anger Management	Page 36
• Anger Management	Solving a Problem	Page 40
• ADHD	Establishing Behavioral Plans	Page 70
• ADHD	Stop and Think	Page 84
• Disruptive Behavior	Weighing the Options	Page 135
• Disruptive Behavior	Communicating Assertively	Page 139
• Oppositional Defiant Disorder	Improved Communication	Page 200
• Oppositional Defiant Disorder	Another Point of View	Page 207
• Oppositional Defiant Disorder	Conflict Resolution	Page 212

ADDITIONAL PROBLEMS FOR WHICH THIS EXERCISE MAY BE USEFUL

• ADHD
• Anger Management
• Conduct Disorder
• Disruptive Behavior
• Oppositional Defiant Disorder

SUGGESTIONS FOR PROCESSING THIS EXERCISE WITH CLIENT

Children who exhibit severe behavioral difficulties frequently are unable to manage their frustration level. They become easily frustrated and act out behaviorally. The severity of the acting-out behavior appears to be greatly exaggerated when looking at the precipitating factors. That is, the child may have an intense negative reaction to a very small event. One goal of therapy is to help the child begin to understand the association between feelings and reactive behaviors. This homework assignment will help the child become more aware of and be able to verbalize feelings of frustration.

Present this homework assignment in the therapy session and request that the child identify situations that have resulted in feelings of frustration. As part of the homework assignment, the child will have to draw three pictures. The first is a picture of the child when he/she was frustrated. The second is a picture of what frustrates the child. The final picture is a drawing of what happens when he/she gets frustrated.

In the next therapy session, review the three drawings and focus on strategies to manage frustration. Discussion should focus on one situation in which the child was frustrated. Identify precipitants of the situation and strategies to manage the situation more effectively.

I'M SO FRUSTRATED I COULD BURST

What do you look like when you are frustrated? Draw a picture of a time when you felt frustrated.

What frustrates you? Draw a picture of one thing that frustrates you.

What happens when you get frustrated? Draw a picture of what usually happens when you get frustrated.

PUTTING IT INTO PERSPECTIVE

GOALS OF THE EXERCISE

1. Become aware of and verbalize feelings.
2. Identify strategies to manage frustration more effectively.
3. Become aware of the association between feelings and reactive behavior.
4. Recognize that difficulties can arise when the severity of the response does not match the situation.

ADDITIONAL HOMEWORK THAT MAY BE APPLICABLE TO CONDUCT DISORDER

• Anger Management	Anger Control	Page 31
• Anger Management	Anger Management	Page 36
• Anger Management	Solving a Problem	Page 40
• ADHD	Establishing Behavioral Plans	Page 70
• ADHD	Stop and Think	Page 84
• Disruptive Behavior	Weighing the Options	Page 135
• Disruptive Behavior	Communicating Assertively	Page 139
• Oppositional Defiant Disorder	Improved Communication	Page 200
• Oppositional Defiant Disorder	Another Point of View	Page 207
• Oppositional Defiant Disorder	Conflict Resolution	Page 212

ADDITIONAL PROBLEMS FOR WHICH THIS EXERCISE MAY BE USEFUL

- ADHD
- Anger Management
- Conduct Disorder
- Disruptive Behavior
- Oppositional Defiant Disorder

SUGGESTIONS FOR PROCESSING THIS EXERCISE WITH CLIENT

Children with a history of conduct disorder frequently have exaggerated reactions to relatively small negative events. For example, a child might interpret a glance from a peer as a threat to fight, or an accidental bump as an intentional attempt to hit. One goal of therapy is to help the child begin to put these situations into perspective—that is, to look at the situation more realistically and not to jump into action.

For this assignment, the child will be encouraged to identify five alternative interpretations for specific events. The ability to consider a variety of interpretations can help the child to begin to identify a range of responses to the situation.

Complete the first example in the therapy session. Help the child identify alternative interpretations for the event. Encourage the child to recognize that a given event can have multiple interpretations. Once the child understands the task, instruct him/her to identify alternative interpretations for the other situations. Review each of the completed worksheets in the therapy session.

PUTTING IT INTO PERSPECTIVE

Sometimes we are certain about someone's motives or intentions and we are absolutely wrong. For example, we might see that a friend looks angry and think that he/she is angry at us, but instead the person is angry about something else. It is important to consider all of the alternatives before jumping to a conclusion about a situation. For each of these situations think of five possible alternatives for the reaction.

When this happens:	It could mean:
A friend in your class makes a face.	1.
	2.
	3.
	4.
	5.

When this happens:	It could mean:
A classmate takes your pencil without asking.	1.
	2.
	3.
	4.
	5.

When this happens:	It could mean:
Someone with whom you do not usually get along smiles at you.	1.
	2.
	3.
	4.
	5.

When this happens:	It could mean:
A stranger bumps into you in school.	1.
	2.
	3.
	4.
	5.

When this happens:	It could mean:
A person in your class looks really mad.	1.
	2.
	3.
	4.
	5.

Section VIII

DEPRESSION

COPING WITH SADNESS

GOALS OF THE EXERCISE

1. Verbalize factors that contribute to depression.
2. Identify precipitants of depression.
3. Express feelings of sadness.
4. Identify strategies to manage depression.

ADDITIONAL HOMEWORK THAT MAY BE APPLICABLE TO DEPRESSION

• Disruptive Behavior	Communicating Assertively	Page 139
• Self-Esteem	Recognizing the Wonderful Things about You	Page 286
• Self-Esteem	Thinking Positively	Page 291
• Self-Esteem	Self-Improvement	Page 296
• Self-Esteem	Fantastic Me	Page 301
• Self-Esteem	Bill of Rights	Page 305
• Self-Esteem	Wishes	Page 308
• Self-Esteem	Goal Setting	Page 313
• Oppositional Defiant Disorder	Improved Communication	Page 200

ADDITIONAL PROBLEMS FOR WHICH THIS EXERCISE MAY BE USEFUL

- Anxiety
- Grief/Loss
- Self-Esteem

SUGGESTIONS FOR PROCESSING THIS EXERCISE WITH CLIENT

Children who have symptoms of depression frequently have difficulty verbalizing their feelings. This homework assignment encourages the child to express feelings of sadness and to begin to identify factors that lead to feelings of sadness. This homework assignment can be divided into three weeks or completed within one week.

Review each worksheet in the therapy session. The first worksheet helps the child become aware of feelings of sadness through having the child draw a picture of a time when he/she felt sad. The second worksheet encourages the child to identify precipitants of sadness and requests that the child identify things that make him/her feel sad. The final worksheet focuses on strategies to manage feelings of sadness. The child can complete this worksheet alone or with the help of the family. In the therapy session, help the child rate the effectiveness of each strategy.

Each of the worksheets should be reviewed in the therapy session and used to help the child use words to begin to verbalize feelings.

COPING WITH SADNESS

Draw a picture of a time when you felt sad.

Things That Make Me Sad

Fill each box with a picture of something that makes you sad.

What Can I Do When I Get Sad?

List 10 things you can do when you get sad.

1. _____

2. _____

3. _____

4. _____

5. _____

6. _____

7. _____

8. _____

9. _____

10. _____

COMMUNICATING FEELINGS

GOALS OF THE EXERCISE

1. Increase the ability to express emotional needs to significant others.
2. Become aware of feelings.
3. Increase the ability to express feelings.

ADDITIONAL HOMEWORK THAT MAY BE APPLICABLE TO DEPRESSION

• Disruptive Behavior	Communicating Assertively	Page 139
• Self-Esteem	Recognizing the Wonderful Things about You	Page 286
• Self-Esteem	Thinking Positively	Page 291
• Self-Esteem	Self-Improvement	Page 296
• Self-Esteem	Fantastic Me	Page 301
• Self-Esteem	Bill of Rights	Page 305
• Self-Esteem	Wishes	Page 308
• Self-Esteem	Goal Setting	Page 313
• Oppositional Defiant Disorder	Improved Communication	Page 200

ADDITIONAL PROBLEMS FOR WHICH THIS EXERCISE MAY BE USEFUL

- Anxiety
- Grief/Loss
- Self-Esteem

SUGGESTIONS FOR PROCESSING THIS EXERCISE WITH CLIENT

Children frequently have difficulty verbalizing feelings. This homework assignment will help the child begin to learn emotional vocabulary. These worksheets should be reviewed with the child and his/her parents/guardian in the therapy session.

For the first page, help the child identify situations in which he/she experienced each feeling. In the next week, the child will review the worksheet with his/her parents/guardian each day and describe how he/she feels that day.

For the second worksheet, the child will draw pictures of times when he/she felt each emotion. Review each emotion in the session to be certain that the child is familiar with

114

each word. Instruct the child to describe or draw a picture of a time when he/she experienced each of the feelings. These two worksheets will help the child begin to express emotions.

The final part of the assignment focuses on verbal communication of feelings. This worksheet will require review in the therapy session. Be certain to role-play situations in which the child can begin to verbally express feelings. Have the child read the worksheet in the session. Role-play a variety of scenarios to help the child communicate feelings. Be sure to role-play situations that involve interactions with peers, siblings, and parents/guardian.

COMMUNICATING FEELINGS

Today I feel . . .

afraid	angry
confused	disappointed
embarrassed	excited
frustrated	guilty
happy	helpless
hopeful	jealous
lonely	loved
mad	nervous
proud	sad
scared	worried

Use words or pictures to describe a time when you felt . . .

afraid	angry
excited	**frustrated**
nervous	**sad**

It is often difficult to tell someone you care about that there is something bothering you. Here are some simple words that can help you communicate how you feel.

By filling in the blanks you can tell someone how you feel in certain situations. Practice using these words to communicate how you are feeling.

When you _____ ,
I feel _____ .

List five situations in which you could use these words to communicate your feelings:

1.

2.

3.

4.

5.

WHAT MAKES YOU HAPPY?

GOALS OF THE EXERCISE

1. Identify strategies to elevate mood.
2. Increase energy, activities, and socialization.
3. Identify strategies to manage depression.

ADDITIONAL HOMEWORK THAT MAY BE APPLICABLE TO DEPRESSION

•	Disruptive Behavior	Communicating Assertively	Page 139
•	Self-Esteem	Recognizing the Wonderful Things about You	Page 286
•	Self-Esteem	Thinking Positively	Page 291
•	Self-Esteem	Self-Improvement	Page 296
•	Self-Esteem	Fantastic Me	Page 301
•	Self-Esteem	Bill of Rights	Page 305
•	Self-Esteem	Wishes	Page 308
•	Self-Esteem	Goal Setting	Page 313
•	Oppositional Defiant Disorder	Improved Communication	Page 200

ADDITIONAL PROBLEMS FOR WHICH THIS EXERCISE MAY BE USEFUL

- Anxiety
- Grief/Loss
- Self-Esteem

SUGGESTIONS FOR PROCESSING THIS EXERCISE WITH CLIENT

This homework assignment will help the child and family identify strategies that can elevate the child's mood by increasing the child's level of energy and the number of pleasurable activities in which the child participates. Review the assignment in the session with both the child and the parents/guardian. The first page encourages the child to draw pictures of things that make him/her happy. He/she can complete the worksheet alone or with the aid of a parent/guardian. For the second half of this assignment the child will need to list or draw people, places, things, or activities that make him/her happy.

Review the assignment with the child in the therapy session. Instruct the child to complete the drawings and bring them to the next session. Once pleasurable activities have been identified, the child can be encouraged to participate in these activities more frequently.

WHAT MAKES YOU HAPPY?

Things That Make Me Happy

Fill each bubble with a picture of something that makes you happy.

Happiness

List or draw people, places, things, and activities that make you happy. Be sure to include at least two things in each space.

People	Places

Things	Activities

WARNING SIGNS

GOALS OF THE EXERCISE

1. Verbalize factors that contribute to depression.
2. Identify precipitants of depression.
3. Express feelings of sadness.
4. Identify strategies to manage depression.

ADDITIONAL HOMEWORK THAT MAY BE APPLICABLE TO DEPRESSION

• Disruptive Behavior	Communicating Assertively	Page 139
• Self-Esteem	Recognizing the Wonderful Things about You	Page 286
• Self-Esteem	Thinking Positively	Page 291
• Self-Esteem	Self-Improvement	Page 296
• Self-Esteem	Fantastic Me	Page 301
• Self-Esteem	Bill of Rights	Page 305
• Self-Esteem	Wishes	Page 308
• Self-Esteem	Goal Setting	Page 313
• Oppositional Defiant Disorder	Improved Communication	Page 200

ADDITIONAL PROBLEMS FOR WHICH THIS EXERCISE MAY BE USEFUL

- Anxiety
- Grief/Loss
- Self-Esteem

SUGGESTIONS FOR PROCESSING THIS EXERCISE WITH CLIENT

Children who are depressed are unaware of the warning signs of depression. Recognition of early depressive symptoms can be an important aspect of treatment. This homework assignment helps the child begin to identify early symptoms of depression. It is important for both the child and the parents/guardian to begin to recognize symptoms of depression. Therefore, this assignment should be reviewed with both the child and the family.

The first part of this assignment involves reviewing symptoms of depression. Next, the child will begin to identify his/her own symptoms of depression. Finally, the child can begin to recognize what to do when he/she identifies symptoms. The symptoms are described in language that is suitable for young children. If the child continues to have difficulty understanding terms, explain the terms in language the child can understand.

WARNING SIGNS

Have you been experiencing any of the following symptoms?

Really sad

Feeling like nothing will ever get better

Hard to concentrate

Hard to make decisions

Annoyed

Think about death

Think about hurting yourself

Hard to fall asleep

Wake up during the night and can't fall back asleep

Eat too much

Not wanting to eat

Have no energy

Do not want to do anything

Hard time getting started with homework

Difficulty getting along with others

Not wanting to do things you once enjoyed

Want to be alone most of the time

Do not want to see friends

Most people have warning signs of when they are becoming depressed. For some, it is that they eat more than usual. Others eat less. For some, it is that they sleep more than usual. Others sleep less.

What are some of your warning signs that you are getting depressed?

Sleep more

Sleep less

Eat more

Eat less

Feel angry

Stay alone

Feel alone

Feel confused

Get irritated easily

When I get really sad, I usually . . .

_____

_____

_____

_____

It might be more helpful if I . . .

_____

_____

_____

_____

Draw a picture of yourself when you are depressed.

REWRITING COGNITIVE DISTORTIONS

GOALS OF THE EXERCISE

1. Increase positive self-talk.
2. Challenge cognitive distortions.
3. Decrease cognitive distortions.

ADDITIONAL HOMEWORK THAT MAY BE APPLICABLE TO DEPRESSION

• Disruptive Behavior	Communicating Assertively	Page 139
• Self-Esteem	Recognizing the Wonderful Things about You	Page 286
• Self-Esteem	Thinking Positively	Page 291
• Self-Esteem	Self-Improvement	Page 296
• Self-Esteem	Fantastic Me	Page 301
• Self-Esteem	Bill of Rights	Page 305
• Self-Esteem	Wishes	Page 308
• Self-Esteem	Goal Setting	Page 313
• Oppositional Defiant Disorder	Improved Communication	Page 200

ADDITIONAL PROBLEMS FOR WHICH THIS EXERCISE MAY BE USEFUL

*   Anxiety
*   Grief/Loss
*   Self-Esteem

SUGGESTIONS FOR PROCESSING THIS EXERCISE WITH CLIENT

One characteristic of depression is the tendency to distort information. A major goal of treatment is to teach the client to challenge cognitive distortions and to increase positive self-talk.

This homework assignment should be used only when the therapist has provided education about cognitive distortions. The child and family should be educated about cognitive theory and strategies for changing cognitive distortions to more realistic statements.

The first step of this assignment is to have the child and family identify negative thoughts. The next step is to focus on rewriting these distortions.

This assignment can aid the child in identifying and challenging irrational beliefs. This assignment is designed for older children and adolescents. Young children will have difficulty with this assignment.

Instruct the child that for each situation he/she will have to identify alternative interpretations. Review the sample in the therapy session. Instruct the child that he/she must complete the worksheet for homework.

REWRITING COGNITIVE DISTORTIONS

Sometimes when we are having a bad day, we have a tendency to see things in a very negative way. It can be very helpful to put these situations in perspective and see them in a more realistic way.

For example, if you do poorly on an exam, a negative interpretation might include sentences such as "I am stupid." A more realistic interpretation might be "I did poorly on this exam, but if I study hard, I can do better."

Rewrite some negative thoughts into more realistic, positive thoughts.

Situation	Negative Thought	Realistic Thought
1.		
2.		
3.		
4.		
5.		

It is important to learn how to rewrite these negative thoughts into more realistic accurate thoughts. For example:

1. Everyone hates me.   →   1. Jane and I do not get along, but I have several close friends.

2. I am stupid.   →   2. I did not do well on my math test, but I can do better if I study more.

3.

4.

5.

6.

7.

8.

9.

Section IX

DISRUPTIVE BEHAVIOR

WEIGHING THE OPTIONS

GOALS OF THE EXERCISE

1. Improve problem-solving skills.
2. Improve the ability to resolve core conflicts that contribute to disruptive behavior.

ADDITIONAL HOMEWORK THAT MAY BE APPLICABLE TO DISRUPTIVE BEHAVIOR

• Anger Management	Solving a Problem	Page 40
• ADHD	Stop and Think	Page 84
• Conduct Disorder	I'm So Frustrated I Could Burst	Page 101
• Conduct Disorder	Putting It into Perspective	Page 106
• Oppositional Defiant Disorder	Improved Communication	Page 200
• Oppositional Defiant Disorder	Conflict Resolution	Page 212
• Peer Conflict	Compromise	Page 218
• Peer Conflict	Reactions	Page 222

ADDITIONAL PROBLEMS FOR WHICH THIS EXERCISE MAY BE USEFUL

- ADHD
- Anger Management
- Conduct Disorder
- Oppositional Defiant Disorder
- Peer Conflict

SUGGESTIONS FOR PROCESSING THIS EXERCISE WITH CLIENT

This homework assignment will help the child improve decision-making skills and resolve core conflicts that contribute to disruptive behavior. Children exhibiting disruptive behavior frequently have poor problem-solving skills. This assignment will begin to teach problem-solving strategies whereby the child considers alternatives prior to making a decision. This assignment may be difficult for young children. Therefore, it is suggested that the worksheet be completed in the session first, using examples. When the child clearly understands the assignment, instruct him/her to complete the worksheet at home. Discuss a decision that a child must make and instruct the child to list pros and cons.

The next worksheet should be completed using the same approach. Review the worksheet in the session, and when the child understands the task, assign the worksheet as part of the homework. This assignment can be completed by the parents/guardian and child together, where the child works with the parents/guardian to solve a problem and consider alternatives before making a decision.

WEIGHING THE OPTIONS

Describe a decision that you must make.

_____

_____

_____

_____

On this scale, describe the pros and cons associated with this decision.

Cons	Pros

Cross out those items on the con list that are not important to you. Circle those items on the pro list that are very important to you.

When you are making a decision, it is important to consider all the relevant information. Briefly describe a decision you face.

_____

_____

_____

_____

What information do you have to make this decision?

_____

_____

_____

_____

What additional information do you need to make this decision?

_____

_____

_____

How will you get this information?

_____

_____

COMMUNICATING ASSERTIVELY

GOALS OF THE EXERCISE

1. Increase the ability to communicate needs assertively.
2. Decrease aggressive communication.

ADDITIONAL HOMEWORK THAT MAY BE APPLICABLE TO DISRUPTIVE BEHAVIOR

• Anger Management	Solving a Problem	Page 40
• ADHD	Stop and Think	Page 84
• Conduct Disorder	I'm So Frustrated I Could Burst	Page 101
• Conduct Disorder	Putting It into Perspective	Page 106
• Oppositional Defiant Disorder	Improved Communication	Page 200
• Oppositional Defiant Disorder	Conflict Resolution	Page 212
• Peer Conflict	Compromise	Page 218
• Peer Conflict	Reactions	Page 222

ADDITIONAL PROBLEMS FOR WHICH THIS EXERCISE MAY BE USEFUL

- ADHD
- Anger Management
- Conduct Disorder
- Oppositional Defiant Disorder
- Peer Conflict

SUGGESTIONS FOR PROCESSING THIS EXERCISE WITH CLIENT

Children exhibiting disruptive behavior frequently have aggressive communication styles. Rather than communicating their needs assertively, they make demands aggressively. This homework assignment encourages the child to consider alternative strategies to manage conflict. In the therapy session, review the difference between passive, aggressive, and assertive responses to various situations. The use of assertive communication can significantly decrease disruptive behavior. Review and practice responses to conflict situations in the session. Utilize role-playing to help the child begin to learn to use more assertive communication when facing conflict.

Review the three scenarios presented in the homework assignment. Review the three types of responses, and instruct the child to illustrate examples of each response. The drawings will help to reinforce learning from the session.

COMMUNICATING ASSERTIVELY

You are in school and the teacher falsely accuses you of not completing a homework assignment.

Draw a picture of a passive response.

Draw a picture of an aggressive response.

Draw a picture of an assertive response.

Your friend borrows your favorite toy and loses it.

Draw a picture of a passive response.

Draw a picture of an aggressive response.

Draw a picture of an assertive response.

Your friend falsely accuses you of lying.

Draw a picture of a passive response.

Draw a picture of an aggressive response.

Draw a picture of an assertive response.

Section X

DIVORCE

COPING WITH DIVORCE

GOALS OF THE EXERCISE

1. Increase ability to communicate feelings associated with the divorce.
2. Educate parents/guardian about ways to help their child cope with the divorce.

ADDITIONAL HOMEWORK THAT MAY BE APPLICABLE TO DIVORCE

• Blended Families	Family Story	Page 88
• Blended Families	Family Crest	Page 94
• Depression	Communicating Feelings	Page 116
• Self-Esteem	Recognizing the Wonderful Things about You	Page 286
• Self-Esteem	Bill of Rights	Page 305
• Self-Esteem	Wishes	Page 308
• Self-Esteem	Goal Setting	Page 313

ADDITIONAL PROBLEMS FOR WHICH THIS EXERCISE MAY BE USEFUL

*   Blended Families
*   Grief/Loss

SUGGESTIONS FOR PROCESSING THIS EXERCISE WITH CLIENT

Divorce can be a traumatic experience for children that results in many changes (sometimes including changes at home, in school, and with peer groups). Frequently children who are verbal and able to communicate feelings are reluctant to talk about divorce for fear that they will be disloyal to their parents.

This homework assignment encourages the child to express feelings associated with the divorce. This assignment is divided into three sections, which can be completed over several weeks.

The first part of this assignment is a sentence completion, which the child can complete in the therapy session if he/she has difficulty reading. If the child has adequate reading and writing skills, he/she can complete this worksheet at home. Instruct the child to complete each sentence and bring the completed sheet to the next session.

The second part of this assignment involves drawing a picture illustrating the changes since the divorce. The child will bring this drawing to the therapy session for discussion.

The third part of this assignment is designed specifically for the parents and reviews strategies to help the child. Review this handout with parents individually or together, depending on the amount of antagonism associated with the divorce.

COPING WITH DIVORCE

Complete each sentence:

1. When I found out that my parents were divorcing, I felt _____
_____

2. Before the divorce, my parents _____
_____

3. I don't understand _____
_____

4. Since the divorce, I _____
_____

5. Since the divorce, my mom _____
_____

6. Since the divorce, my dad _____
_____

7. Marriage is _____
_____

8. When my parents divorced, I was afraid that _____
_____

9. Divorce is _____
_____

10. My parents got divorced because _____
_____

11. One good thing since the divorce is _____
_____

What things have changed at your home since your parents divorced or separated? Draw pictures of some of the changes.

1.	2.
3.	4.

Helping Your Child Cope with Divorce

- Tell your child the facts of the situation in a way that he/she can understand. Be certain that the facts are not too detailed or graphic.

- Allow your child to ask questions and answer these questions honestly. Do not, however, let your own feelings about your ex-spouse influence your answers. When you don't know all the answers, be truthful.

- Be careful not to project your own feelings onto your child.

- Dealing with loss is a process. Do not put pressure on your child to quickly cope with the situation.

- Children who are dealing with loss often fear that they will be abandoned. Reassure your child that you will be there for him/her.

- Allow your child to express his/her feelings.

- Reassure your child that he/she is not responsible for the divorce.

- Do not make promises you cannot keep.

- Take care of yourself. Remember, it is important for you to be there for your child.

- Try to establish a routine and schedule. Your child can gain security from the routine. Often old routines and schedules must change. Therefore, you must establish new traditions and find pleasant activities for your family.

- Try to keep your conflict with your ex-spouse in control. Do not put your child in the center of the conflict.

SINCE THE DIVORCE

GOALS OF THE EXERCISE

1. Increase the ability to communicate feelings associated with the divorce.
2. Educate parents about ways to help their child cope with the divorce.

ADDITIONAL HOMEWORK THAT MAY BE APPLICABLE TO DIVORCE

•	Blended Families	Family Story	Page 88
•	Blended Families	Family Crest	Page 94
•	Depression	Communicating Feelings	Page 116
•	Self-Esteem	Recognizing the Wonderful Things about You	Page 286
•	Self-Esteem	Bill of Rights	Page 305
•	Self-Esteem	Wishes	Page 308
•	Self-Esteem	Goal Setting	Page 313

ADDITIONAL PROBLEMS FOR WHICH THIS EXERCISE MAY BE USEFUL

• Blended Families
• Grief/Loss

SUGGESTIONS FOR PROCESSING THIS EXERCISE WITH CLIENT

Divorce can be a traumatic experience for children that results in many changes (sometimes including changes at home, in school, and with peer groups). Frequently children who are verbal and able to communicate feelings are reluctant to talk about divorce for fear that they will be disloyal to their parents.

This homework assignment encourages the child to verbalize feelings associated with the divorce. The child uses illustrations to tell the story of how he/she found out about the divorce and his/her family after the divorce.

Review the instructions for each of the drawings with the child, and discuss the assignment in the therapy session. These drawings can serve as a springboard for discussion about the divorce and changes in the family. Additionally, these drawings can be used to help the child express feelings in a family session.

SINCE THE DIVORCE

Draw a picture of yourself when you found out about the divorce.

Draw a picture of your family after your parents' divorce.

Section XI

ENURESIS

DECREASING ENURESIS

GOALS OF THE EXERCISE

1. Develop strategies to decrease the child's enuresis.
2. Establish guidelines for parents/guardian to decrease the child's enuresis.

ADDITIONAL HOMEWORK THAT MAY BE APPLICABLE TO ENURESIS

- Anxiety   Stress Management   Page 59
- ADHD   Daily Routine   Page 76

SUGGESTIONS FOR PROCESSING THIS EXERCISE WITH CLIENT

The primary goal of this assignment is to create a behavioral chart that focuses on nocturnal enuresis. The first step involves an accurate assessment of the frequency of enuresis.

During the therapy session, review the behavioral chart with the parents/guardian and child. Inform them that for the first week the child will monitor the number of dry nights on the chart. If the parents/guardian and child can give an accurate assessment of the incidents of enuresis, this step can be omitted. Once a baseline has been established, a behavioral chart can be implemented.

Talk with both the child and the parents/guardian about the bed-wetting and get support from both for the implementation of the behavioral plan. Be certain that the parents/guardian do not intentionally or inadvertently embarrass the child, as this will most likely lead to an increase in enuresis.

Inform the child and parents/guardian that the child will be the monitor of dry mornings. It is imperative for the child to be invested in decreasing enuresis. Often families will unknowingly reward children for enuresis by giving increased attention (albeit negative attention).

Be certain that the expectations for change are reasonable. For example, if a child is bed-wetting nightly, it is unrealistic to expect daily dry nights. The goal for each week should be an increase of one dry night. For example, if the child has three incidents of enuresis in a week, the goal for the next week should be five dry nights.

Inform the child that he/she will maintain the chart. He/she will note dry mornings with a star. Each week the child will share the chart with the outpatient therapist. This chart should *not* be displayed on the refrigerator or shared with all family members. Frequently families of older children begin to organize around the bed-wetting, which can be difficult for the child.

DECREASING ENURESIS

Sunday	Monday	Tuesday	Wednesday	Thursday	Friday	Saturday

TIPS TO DECREASE BED-WETTING

GOALS OF THE EXERCISE

1. Develop strategies to decrease the child's enuresis.
2. Establish guidelines for parents/guardian to decrease the child's enuresis.

ADDITIONAL HOMEWORK THAT MAY BE APPLICABLE TO ENURESIS

- Anxiety   Stress Management   Page 59
- ADHD   Daily Routine   Page 76

SUGGESTIONS FOR PROCESSING THIS EXERCISE WITH CLIENT

Talk with both the child and the parents/guardian about the bed-wetting to get support from both for decreasing it. Be certain that the parents/guardian do not intentionally or inadvertently embarrass the child, as this will most likely lead to an increase in enuresis.

Inform both the child and the parents/guardian that there are certain strategies that significantly decrease enuresis. Parents/guardian may have heard many strategies for this problem and can be skeptical. It is important to reassure the family that this process will be successful.

The first step in any treatment of this problem is to be certain that there is no medical reason for the enuresis. The parents/guardian must schedule a complete physical for the child to rule out any medical reasons for the bed-wetting.

Provide the parents/guardian with the list of suggestions for decreasing enuresis. Review each step carefully with the parents/guardian and the child. It will be important to have the support of both parents/guardian and child.

Instruct the child and parents/guardian about the procedures for wet mornings. The child will be responsible for age-appropriate cleanup. For example, a young child should be responsible for taking off wet clothes, putting them in a designated area, and washing up. Older children can remove sheets and clothes, as well as wash up.

TIPS TO DECREASE BED-WETTING

- Rule out any medical conditions. Schedule an appointment with the primary care physician to be certain that there is no underlying medical condition.

- Do not allow the child to drink any liquids beyond two hours before bedtime. It can be helpful to establish a set time for the intake of the last beverage of the evening. For example, no drinking of liquids after 7:00 p.m.

- The child should go to the bathroom prior to going to sleep.

- Use age-appropriate cleanup. The child should clean himself/herself and place wet clothes in a designated area.

- Do not use diapers.

- Set an alarm clock to wake the child to go to the bathroom. (This strategy should be used temporarily to encourage the child to wake up and go to the bathroom.)

Section XII

FIRE SETTING

FIRE SETTING

GOALS OF THE EXERCISE

1. Decrease fire-setting behavior.
2. Identify dangers associated with fire setting.

ADDITIONAL HOMEWORK THAT MAY BE APPLICABLE TO FIRE SETTING

- Anger Management   Anger Control   Page 31
- Anger Management   Anger Management   Page 36

SUGGESTIONS FOR PROCESSING THIS EXERCISE WITH CLIENT

The primary goal of this assignment is to help the child identify the destructive aspects of fire. Review the assignment with both the child and the parents/guardian. In the therapy session, read the paragraph with the child and instruct him/her to draw a picture of two dangers associated with fire. This drawing can be used to initiate a discussion about the dangers associated with fire setting. The child should also be asked about any personal experiences with fire.

The second part of this assignment involves the child speaking with individuals who have experienced dangers associated with fire. The parents/guardian can help to identify one person who can be interviewed. This person can be a firefighter, a nurse, or someone who has experienced losses associated with a fire. If the child has difficulty writing, the parents/guardian can be the recorder for the interview as the child asks the questions.

FIRE SETTING

Fire is dangerous. Family members and friends can be burned or seriously injured in a fire. People can even die in a fire. Pets can also be burned, seriously injured, or die in a fire. Homes and property can be destroyed.

Draw a picture of two dangers associated with fire.

Interview

Name of person _____

Experience with fire _____
_____

1. What are some of the dangers associated with fire?

   -
   -
   -
   -

2. What can I do to be safe?

   -
   -
   -
   -

GRIEF/LOSS

IT'S HARD TO SAY GOOD-BYE

GOALS OF THE EXERCISE

1. Tell the story of the loss through drawings.
2. Express feelings associated with the loss through art.
3. Develop rapport with the therapist so loss and grief can be discussed.

ADDITIONAL HOMEWORK THAT MAY BE APPLICABLE TO GRIEF/LOSS

• Depression	Coping with Sadness	Page 111
• Depression	Communicating Feelings	Page 116
• Self-Esteem	Wishes	Page 308

ADDITIONAL PROBLEMS FOR WHICH THIS EXERCISE MAY BE USEFUL

- Anxiety
- Depression
- Divorce
- Separation Anxiety

SUGGESTIONS FOR PROCESSING THIS EXERCISE WITH CLIENT

This assignment encourages the child to draw pictures related to the loss. These drawings can be used to initiate discussion about grief and loss in the context of a supportive therapeutic relationship. These drawings can be combined and placed in a folder to create a booklet focusing on changes in the family after the loss.

Five drawings are included in this section:

- The child's family before the loss
- The child and the deceased family member
- A special memory of that special person
- How the child found out about the loss
- The child's family after the loss

These five drawings can be completed over several weeks. Review the instructions with the child in the therapy session. If the child has difficulty reading the worksheets, help the child with the instructions. On each worksheet be sure to fill in the name of the deceased family member. Be certain to use the name that the child used for this family member.

Review each of the drawings with the child. Help the child to verbally express feelings associated with the loss. Children frequently process loss through concrete description of details. When describing how he/she learned about the loss, the child might focus on very specific details. Do not rush the child. Be sensitive to the child's pace for disclosure. The fifth drawing can be used multiple times throughout treatment to help the child understand the stages of loss.

When all of the drawings are complete, compile them to create a booklet. Assemble these drawings in a colored folder that the child can decorate and that will serve as a cover for this personalized booklet about loss. This booklet can be used throughout therapy.

IT'S HARD TO SAY GOOD-BYE

Draw a picture of your family before _____ .

Draw a picture of you and _____ .

Draw a picture of a special memory of you and _____ .

Draw a picture showing how you found out about the loss.

Draw a picture of your family since the loss.

THE LETTER

GOALS OF THE EXERCISE

1. Tell the story of the loss through drawings and writing.
2. Express feelings associated with the loss through art and writing.
3. Develop rapport with the therapist so loss and grief can be discussed.

ADDITIONAL HOMEWORK THAT MAY BE APPLICABLE TO GRIEF/LOSS

- Depression   Coping with Sadness   Page 111
- Depression   Communicating Feelings   Page 116
- Self-Esteem   Wishes   Page 308

ADDITIONAL PROBLEMS FOR WHICH THIS EXERCISE MAY BE USEFUL

- Anxiety
- Depression
- Divorce
- Separation Anxiety

SUGGESTIONS FOR PROCESSING THIS EXERCISE WITH CLIENT

This assignment encourages the child to begin to process feelings associated with the loss. This assignment is divided into three tasks. The first task involves completing several sentences related to the loss. If the child has difficulty writing, this activity can be completed in the therapy session. Instruct the child to complete each sentence.

For the second part of the assignment, the child is asked to draw a picture of the person he/she lost. Instruct the child to bring the drawing to the next therapy session. The therapy session should be used to discuss the drawing and focus on positive memories that the child has about the person.

Using the sentence completion and the drawing, the child can begin to compose a letter to his/her deceased loved one. The child might need assistance to write the letter. The letter should be written in the therapy session. For children who have difficulty writing, the therapist can serve as the recorder as the child dictates the letter.

THE LETTER

Think about _____ and finish the following sentences:

I remember when we _____

_____

_____

I wish _____

_____

_____

I liked it when you _____

_____

_____

I didn't like it when you _____

_____

_____

It was really funny when we _____

_____

_____

I was really sad when _____

_____

_____

I miss _____

_____

_____

Sometimes I think about _____

_____

_____

My favorite memory is when we _____

_____

_____

Draw a picture of _____ .

Dear _____ ,

_____

_____

_____

_____

_____

_____

_____

_____

_____

_____

_____

_____

_____

_____

_____

_____

_____

_____

_____

_____

_____

_____

_____

_____

_____

_____

_____

_____

AS TIME PASSES

GOALS OF THE EXERCISE

1. Understand the stages of grief.
2. Express feelings associated with the loss.
3. Develop rapport with the therapist so loss and grief can be discussed.

ADDITIONAL HOMEWORK THAT MAY BE APPLICABLE TO GRIEF/LOSS

• Depression	Coping with Sadness	Page 111
• Depression	Communicating Feelings	Page 116
• Self-Esteem	Wishes	Page 308

ADDITIONAL PROBLEMS FOR WHICH THIS EXERCISE MAY BE USEFUL

* Anxiety
* Depression
* Divorce
* Separation Anxiety

SUGGESTIONS FOR PROCESSING THIS EXERCISE WITH CLIENT

When dealing with loss it can be helpful for children and families to understand the stages associated with grieving. This homework assignment introduces the child and the family to the stages of grief: denial, anger, bargaining, depression, and acceptance (Kübler-Ross, 1969). Frequently children within a family will be experiencing different stages at different times. This discrepancy can result in conflict between family members when one individual is extremely angry and another is in denial. This assignment briefly introduces the stages of grief and can be used with an individual child or with an entire family. For this assignment, have the child read the short story at home and provide illustrations for each page.

Introduce the child and family to the stages of grief in the therapy session. Instruct the child to complete the homework assignment and bring the drawings to the next therapy session. These drawings can be used to initiate discussion about the loss and feelings associated with the loss.

AS TIME PASSES

When someone we love dies, we can experience different feelings. There are some common feelings that kids and adults can experience. There are five stages of feelings: denial, anger, bargaining, depression, and acceptance. Read the story about Mary and the variety of feelings that she experienced.

Mary's father died. When she learned that he died, she did not believe it. She was in denial. She did not want to think about what had happened and refused to talk to anyone.

Draw a picture of Mary when she is in denial.

After a little while, Mary became very angry. She was furious that her father had died. Draw a picture of Mary in the angry stage.

Later, Mary was hoping that her father would come back to life. She hoped that if she was on her best behavior, her father would return. She was in the bargaining stage.

Draw a picture of Mary in the bargaining stage.

Mary later became depressed. She was so sad she seemed to be numb.
Draw a picture of Mary in the depression stage.

After some time, Mary accepted her father's death. She was still sad sometimes, but she was able to accept the fact that her father had died.

Draw a picture of Mary in the acceptance stage.

MEDICAL ILLNESS

COPING WITH ILLNESS

GOALS OF THE EXERCISE

1. Express feelings associated with the illness through art.
2. Identify enjoyable activities.

ADDITIONAL HOMEWORK THAT MAY BE APPLICABLE TO MEDICAL ILLNESS

• Anxiety	Relaxation	Page 63
• Depression	Coping with Sadness	Page 111
• Depression	Communicating Feelings	Page 116
• Depression	What Makes You Happy	Page 121
• Depression	Warning Signs	Page 125

ADDITIONAL PROBLEMS FOR WHICH THIS EXERCISE MAY BE USEFUL

• Anxiety
• Depression

SUGGESTIONS FOR PROCESSING THIS EXERCISE WITH CLIENT

This assignment is designed for the child who is currently coping with medical illness. The child is encouraged to express feelings associated with the illness. A child with a medical illness often experiences numerous changes (including decrease in energy, inability to participate in previously enjoyable activities, difficulty participating in activities with peers).

The child is asked to draw three pictures for this assignment:

• A picture of himself/herself since the illness
• Changes since the illness
• An activity that the child enjoys

Each of these drawings can be used to initiate discussion about feelings associated with the illness. Instruct the child to complete the drawings at home and bring the drawings to the next session. Review each drawing with the child in the session.

These drawings can also be used to improve communication between the child and his/her parents/guardian.

COPING WITH ILLNESS

Draw a picture of yourself after you became ill.

Draw pictures of some of the things that have changed since you became ill.

Draw a picture of something you enjoy.

I LIKE TO . . .

GOALS OF THE EXERCISE

1. Increase family understanding of the illness.
2. Identify enjoyable activities.
3. Increase participation in age-appropriate enjoyable activities.

ADDITIONAL HOMEWORK THAT MAY BE APPLICABLE TO MEDICAL ILLNESS

ADDITIONAL PROBLEMS FOR WHICH THIS EXERCISE MAY BE USEFUL

- Anxiety
- Depression

SUGGESTIONS FOR PROCESSING THIS EXERCISE WITH CLIENT

Childhood illness has an impact not only on the child but on every member of the family. Therefore, it is critical for the therapist to work with the entire family. One common pattern for a family is to focus intensely on the illness and on protecting the child with the medical illness. In these situations, activities that do not have an impact on the child's health are limited. Certainly, there can be limitations on activities, which are based on medical necessity. This assignment focuses on clear communication between the child and parents/guardian around issues of restrictions.

The first section of this assignment involves the child identifying activities he/she enjoys. In the second section, the child identifies activities he/she would like to do. This section can be used to initiate discussion about loss as well as to begin discussion about medical factors that might limit participation in some activities. These drawings can be used to initiate discussion about losses (e.g., activities once enjoyed that are not possible) and about the potential for parents/guardian to be overprotective (e.g., parents/guardian not allowing a child to participate in safe activities because of fears).

Open communication can also facilitate discussion with doctors about actual restrictions. Communication between medical personnel, parents/guardian, and the child can result in the identification of modifications that can be made for the child so he/she can safely participate in activities.

I LIKE TO . . .

I would like to . . .

- _____
- _____
- _____
- _____
- _____

Draw a picture of something that you like to do.

I would like to . . .

- _____
- _____
- _____
- _____
- _____

Draw a picture of something that you would like to do.

Section XV

MENTAL RETARDATION

INDEPENDENCE

GOALS OF THE EXERCISE

1. Increase client functioning to an age-appropriate level of independence.
2. Employ positive reinforcement of age-appropriate behavior.
3. Develop effective behavioral management skills.

ADDITIONAL HOMEWORK THAT MAY BE APPLICABLE TO MENTAL RETARDATION

• ADHD	Establishing Behavioral Plans	Page 70
• Self-Esteem	Recognizing the Wonderful Things about You	Page 286
• Self-Esteem	Fantastic Me	Page 301
• Self-Esteem	Wishes	Page 308
• Medical Illness	I Like To . . .	Page 185

ADDITIONAL PROBLEMS FOR WHICH THIS EXERCISE MAY BE USEFUL

- ADHD
- Self-Esteem

SUGGESTIONS FOR PROCESSING THIS EXERCISE WITH CLIENT

This homework assignment involves the participation of the parents/guardian and family. Before completing the behavioral assignment, a therapy session should be scheduled with the family to identify the client's current level of functioning. The therapist should review psychological testing and consult with a psychologist if necessary.

The primary goal of this assignment is to assess the current level of functioning and identify areas where progress is needed.

It is imperative for the family to set realistic goals for the child, whereby the child can achieve success and build upon accomplishments. The first step in establishing realistic goals is to identify a current baseline of behavior and skills.

Children with mental retardation struggle with daily living skills. This assignment will focus on the child's adaptive functioning, particularly daily living skills. This process involves measuring baseline skill levels and setting realistic goals. Once the parents/guardian have mastered the behavioral techniques of identifying baseline levels, establishing goals, and developing behavioral charts, these techniques can be used to modify other behaviors.

Instruct the parents/guardian in methods to implement these behavioral techniques. The first step is to determine baseline levels. To establish a baseline for a skill level, ask the parents/guardian to complete the assessment sheet that looks at daily living skills. The parents/guardian should describe the child's skill level in each area.

In the next session the therapist should review the daily living skills worksheets and establish realistic weekly goals for each area. Provide the parents/guardian with instructions about establishing effective goals. Each week a behavioral chart can be created to focus on current behavioral goals.

INDEPENDENCE

Please complete the following sheets, which focus on daily routines. Please describe your child's strengths and limitations in each area.

MORNING ROUTINE

- Get washed
- Brush teeth
- Get dressed
- Prepare breakfast
- Feed self

Strengths

_____

_____

_____

Limitations

_____

_____

_____

AFTER-SCHOOL ROUTINE

- Complete chores
- Complete assignments

Strengths

_____

_____

Limitations

_____

_____

_____

DINNER ROUTINE

Strengths

- Set table
- Feed self
- Clean table

_____

_____

_____

Limitations

_____

_____

_____

BEDTIME ROUTINE

Strengths

- Change into pajamas
- Wash up

_____

_____

_____

Limitations

_____

_____

_____

OTHER AREAS

_____

_____

Goal for This Week

_____

_____

Reward

_____

_____

Behavioral Chart

_____

Monday

_____

Tuesday

_____

Wednesday

_____

Thursday

_____

Friday

_____

Saturday

_____

Sunday

_____

PART OF THE FAMILY

GOALS OF THE EXERCISE

1. Increase the sense of belonging in the family and community.
2. Increase the communication of feelings.

ADDITIONAL HOMEWORK THAT MAY BE APPLICABLE TO MENTAL RETARDATION

• ADHD	Establishing Behavioral Plans	Page 70
• Self-Esteem	Recognizing the Wonderful Things about You	Page 286
• Self-Esteem	Fantastic Me	Page 301
• Self-Esteem	Wishes	Page 308
• Medical Illness	I Like To . . .	Page 185

ADDITIONAL PROBLEMS FOR WHICH THIS EXERCISE MAY BE USEFUL

- ADHD
- Self-Esteem

SUGGESTIONS FOR PROCESSING THIS EXERCISE WITH CLIENT

Families with children with special needs frequently organize around the disability. The goal of this assignment is to help the child develop a sense of acceptance and a feeling of belonging in the family.

This assignment should be completed with the entire family. Instruct the family to complete three drawings:

- Our family
- Our family doing something that we enjoy
- Our family at our favorite place

The drawings can be completed in one week or over several weeks.

The family should bring the drawings to the therapy session and discuss the process of completing the drawings. This task will help the family to focus on the family unit and on enjoyable activities and places.

PART OF THE FAMILY

Our Family

Our Family Doing Something We Enjoy

Our Family at Our Favorite Place

OPPOSITIONAL DEFIANT DISORDER

IMPROVED COMMUNICATION

GOALS OF THE EXERCISE

1. Increase assertive behavior.
2. Verbalize feelings in constructive ways.
3. Develop conflict resolution skills.
4. Develop strategies to manage conflict.

ADDITIONAL HOMEWORK THAT MAY BE APPLICABLE TO OPPOSITIONAL DEFIANT DISORDER

ADDITIONAL PROBLEMS FOR WHICH THIS EXERCISE MAY BE USEFUL

*   ADHD
*   Anger Management
*   Conduct Disorder
*   Disruptive Behavior
*   Peer Conflict

SUGGESTIONS FOR PROCESSING THIS EXERCISE WITH CLIENT

A child who is oppositional has difficulty resolving conflict. This homework assignment can be used to help the child develop basic problem-solving skills.

This assignment should be completed over several weeks. Each week the child should complete one drawing. The drawings focus on how the child responds to a variety of conflict situations.

Review each scenario with the child in the therapy session and role-play problem-solving skills. Focus on the scenario and review the consequences associated with different problem-solving options. In the session, have the child choose the best solution to the problem.

The five drawings can be combined to create a workbook that provides a review of the problem-solving skills.

IMPROVED COMMUNICATION

What Would You Do or Say?

Someone gets in front of you when you are waiting in line. Draw a picture of what you would do or say.

What Would You Do or Say?

Your teacher calls you the wrong name. Draw a picture of what you would do or say.

What Would You Do or Say?

Someone knocks over your drink in the school cafeteria. Draw a picture of what you would do or say.

What Would You Do or Say?

Your parents/guardian forget your allowance. Draw a picture of what you would do or say.

What Would You Do or Say?

A classmate makes fun of you. Draw a picture of what you would do or say.

ANOTHER POINT OF VIEW

GOALS OF THE EXERCISE

1. Increase empathy toward others.
2. Develop conflict resolution skills.
3. Increase the ability to consider multiple alternatives and compromise.

ADDITIONAL HOMEWORK THAT MAY BE APPLICABLE TO OPPOSITIONAL DEFIANT DISORDER

- Anger Management   Anger Management   Page 36
- Anger Management   Solving a Problem   Page 40
- ADHD   Establishing Behavioral Plans   Page 70
- ADHD   Stop and Think   Page 84
- Conduct Disorder   I'm So Frustrated I Could Burst   Page 101
- Conduct Disorder   Putting It into Perspective   Page 106
- Disruptive Behavior   Weighing the Options   Page 135
- Disruptive Behavior   Communicating Assertively   Page 139
- Peer Conflict   Compromise   Page 218
- Peer Conflict   Reactions   Page 222

ADDITIONAL PROBLEMS FOR WHICH THIS EXERCISE MAY BE USEFUL

- ADHD
- Anger Management
- Conduct Disorder
- Disruptive Behavior
- Peer Conflict

SUGGESTIONS FOR PROCESSING THIS EXERCISE WITH CLIENT

Children who are oppositional frequently have difficulty recognizing how their own behavior can escalate a conflict. Minor issues can snowball into major conflicts because of defiance and oppositional behavior. The goal of this assignment is to help the child recognize alternatives and become cognizant of the point of view of others.

Review the entire assignment with the child and use an example to illustrate each step of the task. The homework assignment presents a problem-solving strategy. This assignment can also aid in the development of empathy. The child is encouraged to begin to identify another point of view when resolving a conflict.

Instruct the child that he/she can draw his/her responses or write them out. Younger children might have difficulty writing and can complete this assignment with the assistance of a parent/guardian.

The child should bring the completed worksheet to the therapy session. Review the homework assignment and focus on strategies used to solve the problem.

The therapist can use this assignment multiple times throughout the course of therapy. When a conflict is identified in the therapy session, the child can complete the problem-solving worksheet as a homework assignment.

ANOTHER POINT OF VIEW

When facing a conflict with another individual, it is often very helpful to consider his/her point of view.

Describe or draw a picture of a conflict that you had with another person.

Describe your point of view. How did you feel?

Describe the other person's point of view. How did he/she feel?

CONFLICT RESOLUTION

GOALS OF THE EXERCISE

1. Increase conflict resolution skills.
2. Increase problem-solving skills.
3. Increase empathy.

ADDITIONAL HOMEWORK THAT MAY BE APPLICABLE TO OPPOSITIONAL DEFIANT DISORDER

• Anger Management	Anger Management	Page 36
• Anger Management	Solving a Problem	Page 40
• ADHD	Establishing Behavioral Plans	Page 70
• ADHD	Stop and Think	Page 84
• Conduct Disorder	I'm So Frustrated I Could Burst	Page 101
• Conduct Disorder	Putting It into Perspective	Page 106
• Disruptive Behavior	Weighing the Options	Page 135
• Disruptive Behavior	Communicating Assertively	Page 139
• Peer Conflict	Compromise	Page 218
• Peer Conflict	Reactions	Page 222

ADDITIONAL PROBLEMS FOR WHICH THIS EXERCISE MAY BE USEFUL

- ADHD
- Anger Management
- Conduct Disorder
- Disruptive Behavior
- Peer Conflict

SUGGESTIONS FOR PROCESSING THIS EXERCISE WITH CLIENT

Children frequently need cognitive prompts to understand another person's perspective. It can be even more difficult for children who are frequently oppositional. This assignment will help the child develop problem-solving skills that involve understanding a conflict from another person's perspective.

Children who are oppositional have difficulty resolving conflict with individuals who have a position of authority (e.g., teachers, parents, coaches). These children can benefit from therapy that focuses on problem solving and conflict resolution.

This homework assignment requires the child to systematically think through each aspect of the conflict. For this assignment the child will document what happened at each phase of the conflict. Once each phase of the conflict is described in writing, the child will illustrate each aspect of the conflict.

The written part of this assignment should be completed in the therapy session. Have the child focus on a specific conflict and answer all of the questions on the worksheets. For younger children, the therapist may need to be the recorder and document the child's words. The child will be required to verbally describe the details of the conflict. In the therapy session, help the child to begin to see other ways the conflict can be resolved.

For homework, instruct the child to provide illustrations for each section of the worksheet. This assignment can be used multiple times to help the child develop more effective problem-solving skills.

CONFLICT RESOLUTION

Who was involved in the conflict?

_____

_____

Draw a picture of the people in the conflict.

_____

What started the conflict?

_____

_____

Draw a picture of what started the conflict.

What did you do?

_____

_____

Draw a picture of what you did.

```
┌─────────────────────────────────────────────┐
│                                               │
│                                               │
│                                               │
│                                               │
│                                               │
│                                               │
│                                               │
│                                               │
└─────────────────────────────────────────────┘
```

_____

What did the other person do?

_____

_____

Draw a picture of what the other person did.

```
┌─────────────────────────────────────────────┐
│                                               │
│                                               │
│                                               │
│                                               │
│                                               │
│                                               │
│                                               │
│                                               │
└─────────────────────────────────────────────┘
```

How was the problem resolved?

_____

_____

Draw a picture of how the problem was resolved.

_____

What else could have been done to resolve the problem?

_____

_____

Draw a picture of another solution.

PEER CONFLICT

COMPROMISE

GOALS OF THE EXERCISE

1. Increase empathy toward others.
2. Develop conflict resolution skills.
3. Increase the ability to consider multiple alternatives and compromise.

ADDITIONAL HOMEWORK THAT MAY BE APPLICABLE TO PEER CONFLICT

• Anger Management	Anger Management	Page 36
• Anger Management	Solving a Problem	Page 40
• ADHD	Establishing Behavioral Plans	Page 70
• ADHD	Stop and Think	Page 84
• Conduct Disorder	I'm So Frustrated I Could Burst	Page 101
• Conduct Disorder	Putting It into Perspective	Page 106
• Disruptive Behavior	Communicating Assertively	Page 139
• Oppositional Defiant Disorder	Improved Communication	Page 200
• Oppositional Defiant Disorder	Another Point of View	Page 207
• Oppositional Defiant Disorder	Conflict Resolution	Page 212
• Social Phobia	Making Friends	Page 351

ADDITIONAL PROBLEMS FOR WHICH THIS EXERCISE MAY BE USEFUL

- ADHD
- Anger Management
- Conduct Disorder
- Disruptive Behavior
- Oppositional Defiant Disorder

SUGGESTIONS FOR PROCESSING THIS EXERCISE WITH CLIENT

This homework assignment is designed for children who have difficulty relating to peers. Often these children have limited empathy skills. They have difficulty understanding another person's point of view and relating to peers. When solving problems they frequently focus on their own perspective and do not consider any type of compromise.

The therapist should introduce the assignment in the therapy session. Ask the child to describe a problem or conflict that involves two people. Complete each section of the worksheet with the child.

On the left side of the worksheet describe in writing:

1. The problem
2. The child's solution
3. The solution according to another's point of view
4. A compromise

Instruct the child to provide illustrations in the designated boxes as a homework assignment.

Once the child understands the task, he/she can complete the same worksheet, focusing on another conflict, for homework. In the session, identify a conflict and instruct the child to complete the worksheet as homework and bring it to the next therapy session.

COMPROMISE

When problems involve other people, it is important to consider the other person's point of view. Think of a problem that involves another person.

Describe the problem.   Draw a picture of the problem.

What did you think would solve the problem?

What did the other person think would solve the problem?

Describe how you both could compromise.

Draw a picture of the compromise.

REACTIONS

GOALS OF THE EXERCISE

1. Increase empathy toward others.
2. Increase awareness of one's own reactions to a conflict.
3. Increase awareness of alternatives available in a conflict.
4. Increase awareness that assertive communication can aid in resolving peer conflict.

ADDITIONAL HOMEWORK THAT MAY BE APPLICABLE TO PEER CONFLICT

• Anger Management	Anger Management	Page 36
• Anger Management	Solving a Problem	Page 40
• ADHD	Establishing Behavioral Plans	Page 70
• ADHD	Stop and Think	Page 84
• Conduct Disorder	I'm So Frustrated I Could Burst	Page 101
• Conduct Disorder	Putting It into Perspective	Page 106
• Disruptive Behavior	Communicating Assertively	Page 139
• Oppositional Defiant Disorder	Improved Communication	Page 200
• Oppositional Defiant Disorder	Another Point of View	Page 207
• Oppositional Defiant Disorder	Conflict Resolution	Page 212
• Social Phobia	Making Friends	Page 351

ADDITIONAL PROBLEMS FOR WHICH THIS EXERCISE MAY BE USEFUL

- ADHD
- Anger Management
- Conduct Disorder
- Disruptive Behavior
- Oppositional Defiant Disorder

SUGGESTIONS FOR PROCESSING THIS EXERCISE WITH CLIENT

This two-part homework assignment addresses two issues related to peer conflict. For the first part of this assignment, instruct the child to complete the sentences. This sentence completion focuses on identifying people with whom the child feels comfortable talking. This first part of the assignment should be reviewed in the therapy session. This assignment can be used to initiate discussion about feelings and the importance of assertively communicating one's needs.

For the second part of this assignment, the child will identify his/her own reactions to a variety of settings. The first step in conflict resolution is becoming aware of one's own reaction to the situation. Does the child typically become aggressive or is he/she initially passive and later becomes aggressive? This assignment will help the child become aware of his/her reactions.

The child will complete six drawings that focus on the potential conflict situations. Instruct the child to complete all six drawings and bring the completed assignment to the next session.

In the therapy session, review each drawing and help the child identify possible consequences for each reaction. If the child does not like the consequences, have him/her identify alternative strategies for managing the conflict. The therapy session can be used to role-play these situations.

REACTIONS

Complete the following sentences:

1. I usually talk to _____ .

2. It is hard for me to talk about _____
_____.

3. When I talk to my parent(s)/guardian, _____
_____.

4. When I talk to my best friend, _____
_____.

5. I wish I could talk to _____ .

6. I wish I could talk to someone about _____
_____.

7. When I have a serious problem, I usually talk to _____ .

8. I talk about my feelings to _____
_____.

9. When someone yells at me, I _____
_____.

10. A good listener _____ .

Draw pictures of how you would react in each of the following situations.

A friend teases you

_____

A bigger kid calls you a name

_____

A friend teases another kid in your class

Draw pictures of how you would react in each of the following situations.

A friend says something about you that is not true

_____

A friend is avoiding you

_____

Your friend is angry with you

TEASING

GOALS OF THE EXERCISE

1. Identify effective strategies for coping with teasing.
2. Improve problem-solving skills.
3. Increase the ability to consider multiple alternatives and consequences.
4. Improve conflict resolution skills.

ADDITIONAL HOMEWORK THAT MAY BE APPLICABLE TO PEER CONFLICT

ADDITIONAL PROBLEMS FOR WHICH THIS EXERCISE MAY BE USEFUL

• ADHD
• Anger Management
• Conduct Disorder
• Disruptive Behavior
• Oppositional Defiant Disorder

SUGGESTIONS FOR PROCESSING THIS EXERCISE WITH CLIENT

This assignment is designed for children who are frequently teased. In this homework assignment, the child is encouraged to identify consequences associated with various responses to being teased.

Instruct the child to complete the first page of the assignment and bring it to the therapy session. The child is asked to identify the consequences of various responses to teasing on this worksheet. If a child typically responds in an alternative method, write that response in the blank space.

Review the homework assignment in the session. Read the first worksheet with the child and instruct him/her to identify the consequences associated with each reaction. If the child has difficulty writing a response, he/she can draw a picture.

The homework assignment will be used to complete the problem-solving worksheet in the therapy session. Use the consequences identified in the homework assignment to help the child identify an effective strategy for coping with teasing.

TEASING

It can be really difficult to cope with teasing. There are many reactions that kids have to teasing. Each of these reactions has different consequences.

Describe or draw what would happen if you reacted in the following ways:

Fight →

Tease back →

Tell an adult →

Cry →

Walk away →

Ignore it →

Yell at the person →

Tell the person to stop →

_____→

Problem: You are being teased.

Alternatives: **Consequences:**

1.   1.

2.   2.

3.   3.

4.   4.

5.   5.

6.   6.

What is the best solution?

STOP TEASING ME!

GOALS OF THE EXERCISE

1. Identify effective strategies for coping with teasing.
2. Improve problem-solving skills.
3. Identify strategies to eliminate teasing.
4. Improve conflict resolution skills.

ADDITIONAL HOMEWORK THAT MAY BE APPLICABLE TO PEER CONFLICT

• Anger Management	Anger Management	Page 36
• Anger Management	Solving a Problem	Page 40
• ADHD	Establishing Behavioral Plans	Page 70
• ADHD	Stop and Think	Page 84
• Conduct Disorder	I'm So Frustrated I Could Burst	Page 101
• Conduct Disorder	Putting It into Perspective	Page 106
• Disruptive Behavior	Communicating Assertively	Page 139
• Oppositional Defiant Disorder	Improved Communication	Page 200
• Oppositional Defiant Disorder	Another Point of View	Page 207
• Oppositional Defiant Disorder	Conflict Resolution	Page 212
• Social Phobia	Making Friends	Page 351

ADDITIONAL PROBLEMS FOR WHICH THIS EXERCISE MAY BE USEFUL

- ADHD
- Anger Management
- Conduct Disorder
- Disruptive Behavior
- Oppositional Defiant Disorder

SUGGESTIONS FOR PROCESSING THIS EXERCISE WITH CLIENT

This assignment is designed for both a child who is the victim and a child who is the perpetrator of teasing. It is important for both the child who is teased and the child who is bullying to develop empathy for his/her peers.

Instruct the child that he/she will be creating a cartoon that focuses on teasing and strategies to cope with and eliminate teasing. Read the instructions for this homework assignment in the therapy session. Request that the completed assignment be brought to the next therapy session.

Review the first worksheet in the therapy session, focusing discussion on factors that precipitate teasing and strategies to decrease teasing. For the child who is being teased, the discussion should focus on strategies to cope with teasing. For the child who is teasing others, it is important for the child to begin to understand the impact of the teasing.

The second section of this assignment asks the child to draw a picture of one strategy to manage teasing.

This homework assignment can be used with siblings who tease each other excessively. Each sibling should complete the assignment individually and review the assignment in a joint therapy session.

STOP TEASING ME!

Draw a cartoon that shows a child being teased.

Draw a picture of what the child can do to stop the teasing.

PEER PRESSURE

GOALS OF THE EXERCISE

1. Increase the ability to cope with peer pressure.
2. Improve problem-solving skills.
3. Increase assertive communication.
4. Improve communication with peers.

ADDITIONAL HOMEWORK THAT MAY BE APPLICABLE TO PEER CONFLICT

ADDITIONAL PROBLEMS FOR WHICH THIS EXERCISE MAY BE USEFUL

- ADHD
- Anger Management
- Conduct Disorder
- Disruptive Behavior
- Oppositional Defiant Disorder

SUGGESTIONS FOR PROCESSING THIS EXERCISE WITH CLIENT

Children frequently have difficulty coping with peer pressure. This homework assignment should be completed after a therapy session that focuses on peer pressure. Review the assignment in the therapy session. Show the child that on the left side of the worksheet there are peer pressure statements. On the right side there are empty bubbles for responses. The child is asked to think of responses for each of the peer pressure statements and document them in the bubbles on the right side of the page.

This assignment contains 12 statements divided over three pages. The 12 items can be completed in one week or over the course of three weeks. If completed over several weeks, compile the worksheets to make a small workbook.

Instruct the child to complete the homework assignment and bring it to the next therapy session. To further practice assertive communication, role-play the scenarios with the child. In the therapy session, also focus on the potential consequences of each response. In addition, have the child rate the difficulty that he/she would have in using these responses.

PEER PRESSURE

How would you respond to peer pressure?

Are you chicken?

If you were my friend, you would do it.

Just try it once.

How would you respond to peer pressure?

Please. Please. Please.

You have to do it.

Do you think you are better than me?

Nobody will ever find out.

We won't get caught.

How would you respond to peer pressure?

I thought you were my best friend.

If you don't, I will tell everyone.

If you don't, you won't be part of the group.

This is a great idea. If you don't, I will find someone else.

PEER PRESSURE 2

GOALS OF THE EXERCISE

1. Increase the ability to cope with peer pressure.
2. Increase assertive communication.
3. Improve communication with peers.
4. Improve problem-solving skills.
5. Increase the ability to consider consequences of peer pressure.

ADDITIONAL HOMEWORK THAT MAY BE APPLICABLE TO PEER CONFLICT

ADDITIONAL PROBLEMS FOR WHICH THIS EXERCISE MAY BE USEFUL

- ADHD
- Anger Management
- Conduct Disorder
- Disruptive Behavior
- Oppositional Defiant Disorder

SUGGESTIONS FOR PROCESSING THIS EXERCISE WITH CLIENT

This assignment should follow completion of the first peer pressure assignment. The child will be encouraged to identify possible consequences associated with responding to peer pressure. Eight scenarios are presented, and the child is asked to consider the consequences associated with each response.

Review the instructions with the child and instruct him/her to complete each section of the chart. The first column lists scenarios in which peer pressure is frequently used. The second column asks the child to consider the possible consequences associated with engaging in risky activities. In the final column, the child is asked to write down assertive responses to counter peer pressure.

This assignment contains eight statements divided over four pages. The eight items can be completed in one week or over the course of four weeks. If completed over several weeks, compile the worksheets to make a small workbook.

Instruct the child to complete the homework assignment and bring it to the next therapy session. To further practice assertive communication, role-play the scenarios with the child. In the therapy session, also focus on the potential consequences of each response. In addition, the child can rate the difficulty that he/she would have in using these responses.

PEER PRESSURE 2

A friend asks you to:	If you listen to your friend and participate, what could happen?	Instead, you can say:
Cheat on a test		
Steal from a store		

A friend asks you to:	If you listen to your friend and participate, what could happen?	Instead, you can say:
Smoke		
Skip school		

A friend asks you to:	If you listen to your friend and participate, what could happen?	Instead, you can say:
Write graffiti		
Drink alcohol		

A friend asks you to:	If you listen to your friend and participate, what could happen?	Instead, you can say:
Try drugs		
Tell a lie to a close friend		

Section XVIII

PHYSICAL AND EMOTIONAL ABUSE

MY EXPERIENCE

GOALS OF THE EXERCISE

1. Identify and express feelings connected with the abuse through drawings.
2. Verbally express the experience of the abuse.
3. Rebuild a sense of self-worth and remove the sense of fear, shame, and sadness.
4. Verbalize feelings associated with the abuse.

ADDITIONAL HOMEWORK THAT MAY BE APPLICABLE TO PHYSICAL AND EMOTIONAL ABUSE

• Anger Management	Anger Control	Page 31
• Anger Management	Anger Management	Page 36
• Anxiety	Coping with Anxiety	Page 45
• Anxiety	Relaxation	Page 63
• Self-Esteem	Recognizing the Wonderful Things about You	Page 286
• Self-Esteem	Fantastic Me	Page 301
• Self-Esteem	Wishes	Page 308
• PTSD	Impact	Page 259
• PTSD	Coping with Trauma	Page 264
• PTSD	What Happened?	Page 268

ADDITIONAL PROBLEMS FOR WHICH THIS EXERCISE MAY BE USEFUL

- Grief/Loss
- PTSD
- Sexual Abuse

SUGGESTIONS FOR PROCESSING THIS EXERCISE WITH CLIENT

Physical and emotional abuse can have long-term effects on a child's feeling of self-worth and on future relationships. It is imperative for the therapist to be respectful of the child's feelings and the child's pace for expressing the experience of abuse. Pressuring a child to discuss the abuse and express feelings can revictimize the child.

This assignment is designed for therapists who have experience working with children who have been abused. Working outside of one's clinical expertise can be dangerous to the client and is unethical.

This assignment can help the skilled clinician to work with a child who has a history of physical or emotional abuse. For this assignment, the child will complete three drawings of himself/herself. The first drawing is a picture of the child prior to the abuse. The second drawing is a picture of the child during the abuse. The third drawing is a picture of the child after the abuse.

These drawings will help the child begin to verbalize feelings about the abuse in the therapy session. Instruct the child to complete the three drawings and bring them to the therapy session. The drawings can be used to initiate discussion of feelings associated with the abuse.

The therapist should also use his/her best clinical judgment to determine whether this assignment should be completed in the session instead of as a homework assignment.

MY EXPERIENCE

Draw a picture of yourself before the abuse.

Draw a picture of yourself during the abuse.

Draw a picture of yourself after the abuse.

SAFETY

GOALS OF THE EXERCISE

1. Parents/caregivers will establish appropriate boundaries to ensure the protection of the child.
2. Reinforce support and nurturance for the child from family members.

ADDITIONAL HOMEWORK THAT MAY BE APPLICABLE TO PHYSICAL AND EMOTIONAL ABUSE

• Anger Management	Anger Control	Page 31
• Anger Management	Anger Management	Page 36
• Anxiety	Coping with Anxiety	Page 45
• Anxiety	Relaxation	Page 63
• Self-Esteem	Recognizing the Wonderful Things about You	Page 286
• Self-Esteem	Fantastic Me	Page 301
• Self-Esteem	Wishes	Page 308
• PTSD	Impact	Page 259
• PTSD	Coping with Trauma	Page 264
• PTSD	What Happened?	Page 268

ADDITIONAL PROBLEMS FOR WHICH THIS EXERCISE MAY BE USEFUL

- Grief/Loss
- PTSD
- Sexual Abuse

SUGGESTIONS FOR PROCESSING THIS EXERCISE WITH CLIENT

A major focus of therapeutic work with a child who has been victimized is rebuilding the child's sense of security and safety. Maintaining a sense of safety involves both the child and family members. The first part of this assignment involves working with the parents/guardian. The parents/guardian will complete a worksheet that encourages them to recognize strategies to maintain safety.

The second part of this assignment is designed to help the child communicate situations in which he/she does not feel safe. The therapist should also use his/her best clinical judgment to determine whether this section of the assignment should be completed in the session instead of as a homework assignment. In most situations it will be important to complete this aspect of the assignment in the therapy session.

This assignment should be used only by therapists who have experience working with children who have been abused. Working outside of one's clinical expertise can be dangerous to the client and is unethical.

The final drawing should be completed in the therapy session with the parents/guardian and the child. Working in the session, help the child and family identify strategies to increase feelings of security and safety. The therapist should also encourage discussion about safety and establishing strategies to facilitate communication.

SAFETY

It is critical for all children to feel safe and secure. List 10 ways you can maintain your child's safety.

1. _____

2. _____

3. _____

4. _____

5. _____

6. _____

7. _____

8. _____

9. _____

10. _____

Sometimes I don't feel safe when

_____
_____
_____
_____

Draw a picture of a time when you did not feel safe.

Draw a picture of something you can do when you do not feel safe.

POSTTRAUMATIC STRESS DISORDER

IMPACT

GOALS OF THE EXERCISE

1. Identify how the traumatic event has negatively impacted the client's life.
2. Identify and express feelings associated with the trauma.

ADDITIONAL HOMEWORK THAT MAY BE APPLICABLE TO POSTTRAUMATIC STRESS DISORDER

• Anger Management	Anger Control	Page 31
• Anger Management	Anger Management	Page 36
• Anxiety	Coping with Anxiety	Page 45
• Anxiety	Relaxation	Page 63
• Self-Esteem	Recognizing the Wonderful Things about You	Page 286
• Self-Esteem	Fantastic Me	Page 301
• Self-Esteem	Wishes	Page 308

ADDITIONAL PROBLEMS FOR WHICH THIS EXERCISE MAY BE USEFUL

- Grief/Loss
- Physical and Emotional Abuse
- Sexual Abuse

SUGGESTIONS FOR PROCESSING THIS EXERCISE WITH CLIENT

Trauma can have long-term effects on a child's feeling of self-worth and on development. It is imperative for the therapist to be respectful of the child's feelings and the child's pace for expressing the experience of the trauma.

This assignment should be used only by therapists who have experience working with children who have been traumatized. Working outside of one's clinical expertise can be dangerous to the client and is unethical.

This assignment can help the skilled clinician work with a child who has experienced a traumatic event. In the first section of this assignment, the child is asked to draw two pictures. The first is a picture of himself/herself before the traumatic event. The second is a picture of himself/herself after the traumatic event. In the blank, the child is asked to briefly describe the traumatic event. For the next part of this assignment, the child will be asked to identify things that have changed since the trauma. Instruct the child to think of things that have changed and describe or draw them in each circle.

The therapist should also use his/her best clinical judgment to determine whether this section of the assignment should be completed in the session instead of as a homework assignment. In most situations it will be important to complete this aspect of the assignment in the therapy session.

IMPACT

Draw a picture of yourself before _____ .

Draw a picture of yourself after _____ .

In each circle, draw a picture of something that has changed since _____ .

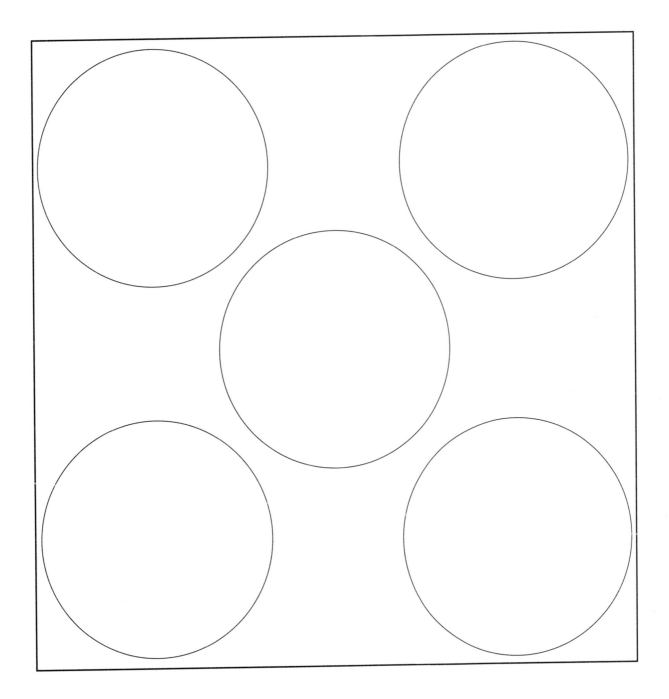

COPING WITH TRAUMA

GOALS OF THE EXERCISE

1. Express feelings associated with the trauma.
2. Draw a picture depicting feelings associated with the trauma.
3. Increase the ability to verbalize feelings associated with the trauma.

ADDITIONAL HOMEWORK THAT MAY BE APPLICABLE TO POSTTRAUMATIC STRESS DISORDER

• Anger Management	Anger Control	Page 31
• Anger Management	Anger Management	Page 36
• Anxiety	Coping with Anxiety	Page 45
• Anxiety	Relaxation	Page 63
• Self-Esteem	Recognizing the Wonderful Things about You	Page 286
• Self-Esteem	Fantastic Me	Page 301
• Self-Esteem	Wishes	Page 308

ADDITIONAL PROBLEMS FOR WHICH THIS EXERCISE MAY BE USEFUL

- Grief/Loss
- Physical and Emotional Abuse
- Sexual Abuse

SUGGESTIONS FOR PROCESSING THIS EXERCISE WITH CLIENT

This assignment can help the skilled clinician work with a child who has experienced a traumatic event. In the first section of this assignment, the child is asked to identify feelings associated with the traumatic event. Instruct the child to fill in the blank and briefly describe the traumatic event.

It is imperative for the therapist to be respectful of the child's feelings and the child's pace for expressing the experience of trauma. Pressuring a child to express feelings can revictimize the child.

This assignment should be used only by therapists who have experience working with children who have been traumatized. Working outside of one's clinical expertise can be dangerous to the client and is unethical.

For the second worksheet, the child will be asked to draw a picture of himself/herself. These worksheets can be used to initiate discussion about the traumatic event and feelings associated with the trauma. The therapist should also use his/her best clinical judgment to determine whether this section of the assignment should be completed in the session instead of as a homework assignment. In most situations it will be important to complete this aspect of the assignment in the therapy session.

COPING WITH TRAUMA

Circle the feelings you have felt since _____ .

afraid

confused

embarrassed

frustrated

happy

hopeful

lonely

mad

proud

scared

angry

disappointed

excited

guilty

helpless

jealous

loved

nervous

sad

worried

Draw a picture of yourself.

WHAT HAPPENED?

GOALS OF THE EXERCISE

1. Increase the ability to describe the traumatic event.
2. Increase the ability to verbalize feelings associated with the trauma.
3. Express facts and feelings associated with the trauma.

ADDITIONAL HOMEWORK THAT MAY BE APPLICABLE TO POSTTRAUMATIC STRESS DISORDER

• Anger Management	Anger Control	Page 31
• Anger Management	Anger Management	Page 36
• Anxiety	Coping with Anxiety	Page 45
• Anxiety	Relaxation	Page 63
• Self-Esteem	Recognizing the Wonderful Things about You	Page 286
• Self-Esteem	Fantastic Me	Page 301
• Self-Esteem	Wishes	Page 308

ADDITIONAL PROBLEMS FOR WHICH THIS EXERCISE MAY BE USEFUL

- Grief/Loss
- Physical and Emotional Abuse
- Sexual Abuse

SUGGESTIONS FOR PROCESSING THIS EXERCISE WITH CLIENT

This assignment can help the skilled clinician work with a child who has experienced a traumatic event. In the first section of this assignment, the child is asked to describe what happened during the traumatic event.

Trauma can have long-term effects on a child's feeling of self-worth and on development. It is imperative for the therapist to be respectful of the child's feelings and the child's pace for expressing the experience of trauma. Pressuring a child to express feelings can revictimize the child.

As with all areas of clinical work, it is important that the therapist have experience working with children who have been traumatized. Working outside of one's clinical expertise can be dangerous to the client and is unethical.

266

For the second worksheet, the child will be asked to draw a picture of himself/herself during the trauma. The therapist can use this drawing to help the child express facts and feelings associated with the trauma.

The therapist should also use his/her best clinical judgment to determine whether this section of the assignment should be completed in the session instead of as a homework assignment. In most situations it will be important to complete this aspect of the assignment in the therapy session.

EXERCISE XIX.C

WHAT HAPPENED?

_____

_____

_____

_____

_____

_____

_____

_____

_____

_____

_____

_____

_____

_____

_____

_____

_____

_____

_____

_____

_____

_____

_____

_____

_____

_____

268

Draw a picture of yourself and what happened.

SCHOOL REFUSAL

I'M GOING TO SCHOOL

GOALS OF THE EXERCISE

1. Identify anxiety-provoking situations associated with school attendance.
2. Obtain information to implement a systematic desensitization program to help the child manage his/her anxiety and gradually attend school for longer periods of time.
3. Obtain information to develop a plan for attending school for increasingly long periods of time.

ADDITIONAL HOMEWORK THAT MAY BE APPLICABLE TO SCHOOL REFUSAL

ADDITIONAL PROBLEMS FOR WHICH THIS EXERCISE MAY BE USEFUL

- Academic Achievement
- Anxiety

SUGGESTIONS FOR PROCESSING THIS EXERCISE WITH CLIENT

This assignment is designed for children who are reluctant to attend school because of anxiety and fears. Based on systematic desensitization, this assignment will help the child identify sources of anxiety and will be used to create a behavioral plan to reduce anxiety.

In the therapy session, introduce the concept of systematic desensitization and describe the technique to the child. The child will complete the homework assignment to identify anxiety-provoking and positive situations at school. This list of anxiety-provoking situations can be used to create the hierarchy of anxiety-provoking situations.

This homework assignment is divided into three sections. Review each section with the child. First, instruct the child to rate the anxiety level associated with each situation and add other situations to the worksheet. The child should rate the anxiety level from 0 (not anxious) to 3 (extremely anxious). The situations are broadly defined and experienced by most children. If the child does not experience a given situation he/she should rate it a 0. For example, if he/she does not have an art class, rate it a 0.

This assignment will help the child begin to identify anxiety-provoking situations in school and also recognize that not all situations are stressful. Using the information gathered in this assignment, the therapist can create a behavioral plan to increase school attendance.

For the second part of this assignment, the child will draw a picture of a very stressful school situation. Instruct the child to draw a picture of a time in school when he/she felt nervous or afraid.

Finally, instruct the child to think of some fun times in school. On the final worksheet the child will draw a picture of a positive school experience.

I'M GOING TO SCHOOL

Rate how nervous or anxious you feel in each situation:

0 = not anxious   1 = a little anxious   2 = medium anxious   3 = very anxious

Getting ready for school	0	1	2	3
Going to school	0	1	2	3
Waiting for school to start	0	1	2	3
Walking into school	0	1	2	3
Walking into the classroom	0	1	2	3
Sitting at your desk in class	0	1	2	3
Gym	0	1	2	3
Recess	0	1	2	3
Lunchtime	0	1	2	3
Reading class	0	1	2	3
Math class	0	1	2	3
Computer class	0	1	2	3
Music class	0	1	2	3
Art class	0	1	2	3

Draw a picture of a time in school when you were nervous.

Draw a picture of something that you enjoy in school.

POSITIVELY SCHOOL

GOALS OF THE EXERCISE

1. Decrease the frequency of negative comments about attending school.
2. Identify positive aspects about school.

ADDITIONAL HOMEWORK THAT MAY BE APPLICABLE TO SCHOOL REFUSAL

- Academic Achievement   School Communication   Page 4
- Academic Achievement   School Is Okay   Page 6
- Academic Achievement   Homework   Page 11
- Self-Esteem   Recognizing the Wonderful   Page 286
                         Things about You
- Self-Esteem   Thinking Positively   Page 291

ADDITIONAL PROBLEMS FOR WHICH THIS EXERCISE MAY BE USEFUL

- Academic Achievement
- Anxiety
- Depression

SUGGESTIONS FOR PROCESSING THIS EXERCISE WITH CLIENT

Frequently a child who refuses to attend school has an extremely negative view about school attendance. The child begins to focus exclusively on negative experiences and fails to recognize positive aspects about school attendance. This homework assignment encourages the child to focus on positive aspects about school.

Review the assignment with the child in the therapy session. Instruct him/her to complete the assignment and bring it to the next therapy session. For this assignment the child will have to identify three aspects about school that he/she enjoys. Ask the child to draw a picture of (1) his/her favorite person at school, (2) a favorite activity at school, and (3) a favorite place at school. It may be helpful to identify these three factors in the therapy session and have the child complete the illustrations at home.

This assignment can also be used to help the child identify allies at the school.

POSITIVELY SCHOOL

My Favorite Person at School

My Favorite Activity at School

My Favorite Place at School

SCHOOL IN VIEW

GOALS OF THE EXERCISE

1. Express feelings about attending school.
2. Express fears associated with school attendance.

ADDITIONAL HOMEWORK THAT MAY BE APPLICABLE TO SCHOOL REFUSAL

ADDITIONAL PROBLEMS FOR WHICH THIS EXERCISE MAY BE USEFUL

*   Academic Achievement
*   Anxiety

SUGGESTIONS FOR PROCESSING THIS EXERCISE WITH CLIENT

Children who experience anxiety related to school attendance frequently have difficulty verbalizing feelings of anxiety. This assignment can help the child begin to express feelings of anxiety.

Children frequently are able to express feelings in drawings and can utilize these drawings to begin to verbalize feelings. This assignment consists of two drawings associated with school. The first assignment has the child draw a picture of himself/herself at school. The trained clinician can evaluate the drawing for factors related to school stressors (i.e., analysis of color, drawing style, location, and content).

Instruct the child to bring the drawing to the next therapy session. The drawing can be used as a springboard for discussion about school, classes, and peer interactions. As the child talks about his/her drawing, begin to focus on factors that are anxiety provoking. The therapy session can be used to uncover the reason for school refusal (anxiety about academic performance, peer conflict, social phobia, separation anxiety).

The second drawing can be completed the next week. Instruct the child to think about a time when he/she was nervous and to draw a picture illustrating that time.

SCHOOL IN VIEW

Draw a picture of you at school.

Draw a picture of a time at school when you were unhappy or nervous.

SELF-ESTEEM

RECOGNIZING THE WONDERFUL THINGS ABOUT YOU

GOALS OF THE EXERCISE

1. Increase self-esteem.
2. Increase self-awareness.
3. Improve self-image.
4. Establish rapport with the child during the early stages of therapy.

ADDITIONAL HOMEWORK THAT MAY BE APPLICABLE TO SELF-ESTEEM

• Anger Management	Solving a Problem	Page 40
• Anxiety	Relaxation	Page 63
• Depression	What Makes You Happy?	Page 121
• Peer Conflict	Teasing	Page 227
• Peer Conflict	Peer Pressure	Page 236
• Peer Conflict	Peer Pressure 2	Page 241

ADDITIONAL PROBLEMS FOR WHICH THIS EXERCISE MAY BE USEFUL

- Anxiety
- Depression
- Peer Conflict

SUGGESTIONS FOR PROCESSING THIS EXERCISE WITH CLIENT

This activity can be used in the early stages of therapy to help the therapist develop rapport with the child. Additionally, this activity can be reviewed with the parents/guardian and the child to help the parents/guardian focus on the child's positive characteristics.

In this exercise the child is asked to complete three drawings that focus on positive characteristics and times when he/she was proud. The instructions for each of the drawings should be reviewed with both the child and the parents/guardian in the therapy session. The child is instructed to bring the drawings to the next session for processing. If the child is able to read, have him/her read the written material. If not, read the worksheets with the child and review the instructions. (Parents/guardian may also need to help the child with reading when completing the assignment.)

In discussing the drawings, you can help the child identify additional positive characteristics. When processing the worksheets, focus discussion on the child's positive characteristics, talents, and skills. Help the child to make "I" statements and be certain that the child does not underestimate his/her strengths. The three worksheets can be combined with other worksheets in this section to make a small booklet that can be shared with the parents/guardian.

RECOGNIZING THE WONDERFUL THINGS ABOUT YOU

Everyone Is Special

This assignment will help your therapist learn more about you.

Draw a picture of yourself on this page. Think of five things about you that are special. Write your special talents and skills on the lines.

_____

_____

_____

_____

Think about a time when you were very proud of yourself. Draw a picture of a time when you were proud.

Draw a picture of yourself doing something that you enjoy.

THINKING POSITIVELY

GOALS OF THE EXERCISE

1. Increase self-esteem.
2. Increase self-awareness.
3. Improve self-image.
4. Establish rapport with the child during the early stages of therapy.
5. Help the parents/guardian identify positive characteristics of the child.

ADDITIONAL HOMEWORK THAT MAY BE APPLICABLE TO SELF-ESTEEM

• Anger Management	Solving a Problem	Page 40
• Anxiety	Relaxation	Page 63
• Depression	What Makes You Happy?	Page 121
• Peer Conflict	Teasing	Page 227
• Peer Conflict	Peer Pressure	Page 236
• Peer Conflict	Peer Pressure 2	Page 241

ADDITIONAL PROBLEMS FOR WHICH THIS EXERCISE MAY BE USEFUL

-   Anxiety
-   Depression
-   Peer Conflict

SUGGESTIONS FOR PROCESSING THIS EXERCISE WITH CLIENT

This homework assignment can be used in the early stages of therapy to begin to develop rapport with the child. Additionally, this assignment can be used with family members so the family can verbally express the child's positive characteristics.

Each of these worksheets can be completed by the child individually or together with the parents/guardian. The benefit of having the parents/guardian assist in completing the assignment is that they can reinforce messages about positive characteristics and thinking positively.

This assignment includes three worksheets that encourage the child to identify positive characteristics about himself/herself. Instruct the child to complete the worksheet at home and bring the completed assignment to the next session.

Review the homework assignment with the child and parents/guardian in the therapy session. The completed assignment can be combined to create a booklet that focuses on the positive aspects of the client.

THINKING POSITIVELY

Circle the words that best describe you:

able to solve problems

artistic

athletic

attractive

confident

creative

dependable

friendly

funny

get along well with others

good listener

hard worker

helpful

intelligent

kind

make others laugh

popular

In each box, draw one positive thing about you.

Favorites

List your favorite:

Place _____

Song _____

Sport _____

Subject _____

Friend _____

Food _____

Movie _____

TV show _____

Hobby _____

Game _____

Sport _____

Color _____

Book _____

Teacher _____

SELF-IMPROVEMENT

GOALS OF THE EXERCISE

1. Improve self-esteem.
2. Express positive characteristics about himself/herself.
3. Express weaknesses and set realistic goals about self-improvement.

ADDITIONAL HOMEWORK THAT MAY BE APPLICABLE TO SELF-ESTEEM

• Anger Management	Solving a Problem	Page 40
• Anxiety	Relaxation	Page 63
• Depression	What Makes You Happy?	Page 121
• Peer Conflict	Teasing	Page 227
• Peer Conflict	Peer Pressure	Page 236
• Peer Conflict	Peer Pressure 2	Page 241

ADDITIONAL PROBLEMS FOR WHICH THIS EXERCISE MAY BE USEFUL

- Anxiety
- Depression
- Peer Conflict

SUGGESTIONS FOR PROCESSING THIS EXERCISE WITH CLIENT

Children with low self-esteem frequently exaggerate negative characteristics. Any imperfection is perceived as a major character flaw. This homework assignment focuses on gaining perspective about negative traits and is designed for older children who have some insight into their own personality traits.

In the first section of this assignment, the child is asked to identify his/her five best traits. The child is also asked to identify two things he/she would like to change about himself/herself. The child should complete this worksheet at home and bring the completed assignment to the therapy session.

The next section of the assignment should be completed in the therapy session. The child will focus on one aspect of himself/herself that he/she would like to change. Children frequently exaggerate negative characteristics. The child will begin to look at this personality trait in greater detail. The therapist should ask questions that allow the child to realistically look at areas for improvement and set realistic goals for change. Help the child see how global generalizations can be incorrect. Instead, the child should identify specific strategies for self-improvement.

The child can complete the last page as a homework assignment. In the session ask the child to identify one aspect of himself/herself that he/she would like to change. For homework, the child will identify three strategies to initiate change.

This homework assignment can be completed over several weeks and should be reviewed in the therapy session. Review the homework assignment with both the child and the parents/guardian. It is important to include the parents/guardian in the session to help them become aware of the child's insecurities. Additionally, the parents/guardian will become more aware of situations in which they criticize the child and when the child interprets comments as negative statements.

SELF-IMPROVEMENT

My best traits:

1.

2.

3.

4.

5.

Two things I would like to change about myself:

1.

2.

Describe or draw a picture of something about yourself that you do not like:

With the help of an adult, consider the evidence. Are you being realistic?

Supporting evidence

Contrary evidence

List one thing about yourself that you would like to change:

_____

_____

With the help of an adult, identify three things that can help you change:

1. _____

_____

2. _____

_____

3. _____

_____

What can you do this week to change?

_____

_____

FANTASTIC ME

GOALS OF THE EXERCISE

1. Increase self-esteem.
2. Express positive characteristics about himself/herself.
3. Express realistic goals about self-improvement.

ADDITIONAL HOMEWORK THAT MAY BE APPLICABLE TO SELF-ESTEEM

• Anger Management	Solving a Problem	Page 40
• Anxiety	Relaxation	Page 63
• Depression	What Makes You Happy?	Page 121
• Peer Conflict	Teasing	Page 227
• Peer Conflict	Peer Pressure	Page 236
• Peer Conflict	Peer Pressure 2	Page 241

ADDITIONAL PROBLEMS FOR WHICH THIS EXERCISE MAY BE USEFUL

- Anxiety
- Depression
- Peer Conflict

SUGGESTIONS FOR PROCESSING THIS EXERCISE WITH CLIENT

This homework assignment encourages the child to identify and record positive attributes. Children with low self-esteem frequently dismiss compliments or statements that focus on positive traits.

This assignment is divided into two sections. Read the instructions with the child and direct him/her to make a list of all his/her positive traits and/or talents. Start the assignment by stating that you will help with creating the list by giving the first example. State one of the child's positive traits.

For the second part of this assignment, read the short instructions in the session and instruct the child to draw two pictures during the next week: one that illustrates a situation in which the child felt bad about himself/herself and one that illustrates a situation in which the child felt good about himself/herself.

Instruct the child to bring the assignment to the next session and review it with the child. This assignment can encourage discussion about precipitants of self-critical behavior. Review this assignment with the parents/guardian to reinforce identification of positive traits. In the session, discuss the importance of reducing the frequency of statements that criticize or demean the child.

FANTASTIC ME

Sometimes when we are feeling down, it is hard to think about our positive traits. At these times, our friends and family can serve as a mirror, by reminding us of our talents and strengths.

Make a list of all of your strengths. Remember all of the positive things your friends and family have ever said about you. Be sure to get input from family and friends to complete the entire list.

1. _____

2. _____

3. _____

4. _____

5. _____

6. _____

7. _____

8. _____

9. _____

10. _____

The things that happen to us during the day often have an impact on our feelings about ourselves. For example, when someone criticizes us, we may feel upset. Or when we get a compliment, we may be proud.

Draw a picture of one situation that resulted in you feeling bad about yourself.

Draw a picture of one situation that resulted in you feeling good about yourself.

BILL OF RIGHTS

GOALS OF THE EXERCISE

1. Increase self-esteem.
2. Increase self-awareness.
3. Improve self-image.
4. Establish rapport with the child during the early stages of therapy.
5. Develop a personal bill of rights.

ADDITIONAL HOMEWORK THAT MAY BE APPLICABLE TO SELF-ESTEEM

- Anger Management   Solving a Problem   Page 40
- Anxiety   Relaxation   Page 63
- Depression   What Makes You Happy?   Page 121
- Peer Conflict   Teasing   Page 227
- Peer Conflict   Peer Pressure   Page 236
- Peer Conflict   Peer Pressure 2   Page 241

ADDITIONAL PROBLEMS FOR WHICH THIS EXERCISE MAY BE USEFUL

- Anxiety
- Depression
- Peer Conflict

SUGGESTIONS FOR PROCESSING THIS EXERCISE WITH CLIENT

This homework assignment focuses on personal awareness and rights. Self-esteem is closely related to self-awareness and respect for one's own rights.

The concepts in this exercise may be difficult for young children to understand. It is critical to review the assignment in the therapy session with both the child and the parents/guardian. This assignment can improve communication between the child and parents/guardian, which is often critical to the development of self-esteem.

On the first worksheet, the child is asked to complete sentences that focus on issues related to self-esteem. Next, the child will create a personal bill of rights. This assignment is particularly difficult for young children. Therefore, this section of the assignment should be completed by the parents/guardian and child together.

Instruct the child and parents/guardian to complete the statement, "I have the right to . . .".

The parents/guardian can also work to create a family bill of rights.

BILL OF RIGHTS

Complete the following sentences:

I am good at _____ .

My greatest strength is my ability to _____ .

I need help with _____ .

I enjoy _____ .

My friends think that I am a good _____ .

My family thinks that I am a good _____ .

A habit that I would like to change is _____ .

In school, I am good at _____ .

I am most proud of _____ .

I am not proud of _____ .

I enjoy _____ with my family.

I enjoy _____ with my friends.

My teachers think that I am _____ .

I am looking forward to _____ .

My happiest memory is _____ .

My saddest memory is _____ .

The best thing about being my age is _____ .

The worst thing about being my age is _____ .

Write your own personal bill of rights.

I have the right to:

* _____
  _____

* _____
  _____

* _____
  _____

* _____
  _____

* _____
  _____

* _____
  _____

* _____
  _____

* _____
  _____

* _____
  _____

* _____
  _____

* _____
  _____

* _____
  _____

* _____
  _____

WISHES

GOALS OF THE EXERCISE

1. Increase self-esteem.
2. Increase self-awareness.
3. Improve self-image.
4. Establish rapport with the child during the early stages of therapy.

ADDITIONAL HOMEWORK THAT MAY BE APPLICABLE TO SELF-ESTEEM

• Anger Management	Solving a Problem	Page 40
• Anxiety	Relaxation	Page 63
• Depression	What Makes You Happy?	Page 121
• Peer Conflict	Teasing	Page 227
• Peer Conflict	Peer Pressure	Page 236
• Peer Conflict	Peer Pressure 2	Page 241

ADDITIONAL PROBLEMS FOR WHICH THIS EXERCISE MAY BE USEFUL

- Anxiety
- Depression
- Peer Conflict

SUGGESTIONS FOR PROCESSING THIS EXERCISE WITH CLIENT

This homework assignment encourages the child to express three wishes each for himself/herself, for family, and for a friend. Complete the written part of this assignment in the therapy session and instruct the child to complete the drawings as homework.

Inform the child that he/she cannot wish for more wishes. Encouraging the child to express wishes can provide insight into goal setting as well as help the therapist identify the child's interests, desires, and wants. The therapy session can be used to further discuss issues related to the three wishes.

This assignment can be completed multiple times during the course of therapy as a gauge of the child's current wishes.

WISHES

Imagine you are granted nine wishes: three for you, three for your family, and three for a friend. What would you wish for yourself?

1. _____

2. _____

3. _____

Draw a picture of yourself with one of your wishes granted.

What would you wish for your family?

1. _____

2. _____

3. _____

Draw a picture of your family with one of your wishes granted.

What would you wish for a friend (name _____)?

1. _____

2. _____

3. _____

Draw a picture of your friend with one of your wishes granted.

GOAL SETTING

GOALS OF THE EXERCISE

1. Increase self-esteem.
2. Increase self-awareness.
3. Improve self-image.
4. Establish rapport with the child during the early stages of therapy.
5. Involve the child in the goal-setting process.

ADDITIONAL HOMEWORK THAT MAY BE APPLICABLE TO SELF-ESTEEM

• Anger Management	Solving a Problem	Page 40
• Anxiety	Relaxation	Page 63
• Depression	What Makes You Happy?	Page 121
• Peer Conflict	Teasing	Page 227
• Peer Conflict	Peer Pressure	Page 236
• Peer Conflict	Peer Pressure 2	Page 241

ADDITIONAL PROBLEMS FOR WHICH THIS EXERCISE MAY BE USEFUL

- Anxiety
- Depression
- Peer Conflict

SUGGESTIONS FOR PROCESSING THIS EXERCISE WITH CLIENT

Children with low self-esteem sometimes have difficulty establishing realistic goals. They can set extremely high standards for themselves and be self-critical or depressed and fail to set goals because of negative thoughts.

Effectively setting and reaching goals is a skill that can be used throughout the child's life. This worksheet can be used multiple times in therapy.

The primary goal of this assignment is to help the child identify a long-term goal and establish steps toward achieving the goal. Because this task can be difficult for young children, it is necessary to read the instructions and complete a sample in the therapy session. It might be helpful to have several copies of the goal worksheet in the session. Complete the assignment in the session using a sample goal.

The sample provided for the therapy session lists the long-range goal "Improve reading level by one grade." Using the worksheet, help the child break the goal into realistic short-term goals. Complete this sample worksheet in the therapy session and, if necessary, complete an additional sample in the session. The development of a goals sheet can be completed in the therapy session or assigned as a homework task for the older child, who will complete the goals sheet and review it in the next session.

For younger children, the goals can be established in the session, and the homework assignment is then to complete the weekly task toward achieving the goal and report on the status in the next therapy session.

GOAL SETTING

Long-term goal: Improve reading level by one grade.
List the steps to reach the goal (design the steps toward reaching the long-term
  goal):

Step #5

_____

_____

Step #4

_____

_____

Step #3

_____

_____

Step #2

_____

_____

Step #1

_____

_____

Reaching a goal can be like climbing steps—you need to go one step at a time to reach the top.

List a goal that you have: _____

_____

List the steps to reach the goal:

Step #5

_____

_____

Step #4

_____

_____

Step #3

_____

_____

Step #2

_____

_____

Step #1

_____

_____

Section XXII

SEPARATION ANXIETY

I CAN DO IT MYSELF

GOALS OF THE EXERCISE

1. Identify strategies for coping with anxiety.
2. Explore the irrational cognitive messages that produce anxiety.
3. Increase the awareness that fears are irrational and/or unrealistic. Improve the ability to examine experiences objectively regarding the low probability of danger, harm, or other feared consequence.
4. Assist in developing reality-based cognitive messages that increase self-confidence to cope with anxiety.
5. Develop positive self-talk as a means of managing anxiety or fears associated with separation.

ADDITIONAL HOMEWORK THAT MAY BE APPLICABLE TO SEPARATION ANXIETY

• Anxiety	Coping with Anxiety	Page 45
• Anxiety	Unrealistic Fears	Page 51
• Anxiety	Managing Anxiety	Page 55
• Anxiety	Stress Management	Page 59
• Anxiety	Relaxation	Page 63
• Depression	Rewriting Cognitive Distortions	Page 130
• Self-Esteem	Thinking Positively	Page 291
• Self-Esteem	Wishes	Page 308

ADDITIONAL PROBLEMS FOR WHICH THIS EXERCISE MAY BE USEFUL

- Depression
- Self-Esteem
- Social Phobia
- Specific Phobia

SUGGESTIONS FOR PROCESSING THIS EXERCISE WITH CLIENT

This homework assignment is designed for children who have unrealistic fears associated with separation from their parents/guardian. The first step of this assignment involves identifying current fears. Children frequently have irrational fears associated with parents/guardian leaving them. Therapy can be used to identify these fears and objectively examine the probability of the feared consequences actually happening.

This assignment can begin in the therapy session. Encourage the child to verbalize fears associated with separation. Write the fears that the child identifies on each of the blank lines on the worksheet. Instruct the child to draw a picture to illustrate each fear.

The next page of this assignment should be introduced in the session and completed at home. Copy the four fears identified in the first section on the next worksheet. For homework, the child will need to gather information that supports or refutes each fear. In the session, describe sources for the evidence (i.e., past experience, interview with parents/guardian). Instruct the child to use multiple sources including parents/guardian and other sources. The child should bring the completed worksheet to the therapy session for review.

I CAN DO IT MYSELF

Sometimes I am afraid that . . .

1. _____

2. _____

3. _____

4. _____

List the evidence suggesting that your fears are not accurate.

1. _____

    evidence: _____

    _____

    _____

2. _____

    evidence: _____

    _____

    _____

3. _____

    evidence: _____

    _____

    _____

4. _____

    evidence: _____

    _____

    _____

FUN WITH FRIENDS

GOALS OF THE EXERCISE

1. Increase participation in extracurricular or peer group activities
2. Improve social skills with peers.

ADDITIONAL HOMEWORK THAT MAY BE APPLICABLE TO SEPARATION ANXIETY

ADDITIONAL PROBLEMS FOR WHICH THIS EXERCISE MAY BE USEFUL

- Depression
- Self-Esteem
- Social Phobia
- Specific Phobia

SUGGESTIONS FOR PROCESSING THIS EXERCISE WITH CLIENT

Children who have difficulty with separation anxiety frequently do not have the opportunity to enjoy peer activities because they are anxious about separation from their parents/guardian. This anxiety can have an impact on peer relationships. This assignment encourages the child to identify a fun activity, participate in a peer activity, and illustrate the event.

This assignment starts within the therapy session. The child, with the assistance of his/her parents/guardian, will identify an activity that can be scheduled with peers. In the session, review the plans for the social activity and focus on positive aspects of this event. Review all aspects of the event with specific details of what will happen—for example: "At 2:00 we will go to Johnny's to go swimming."

Within 48 hours of the activity, the child will need to draw a picture of the peer activity. The child should bring his/her drawing to the therapy session to facilitate discussion about the event. The therapist can also focus on any difficulties associated with the event and role-play solutions. This assignment can be repeated multiple times until the child participates in a peer activity without his/her parents/guardian being present.

FUN WITH FRIENDS

Draw a picture of you and your friend.

SEPARATION FEELINGS

GOALS OF THE EXERCISE

1. Increase the awareness of feelings associated with separation.
2. Increase the ability to verbalize feelings of anxiety.
3. Explore the irrational cognitive messages that produce anxiety.
4. Increase the awareness that fears are irrational and/or unrealistic. Increase the ability to examine the experience objectively regarding the low probability of danger, harm, or other feared consequences.

ADDITIONAL HOMEWORK THAT MAY BE APPLICABLE TO SEPARATION ANXIETY

• Anxiety	Coping with Anxiety	Page 45
• Anxiety	Unrealistic Fears	Page 51
• Anxiety	Managing Anxiety	Page 55
• Anxiety	Stress Management	Page 59
• Anxiety	Relaxation	Page 63
• Depression	Rewriting Cognitive Distortions	Page 130
• Self-Esteem	Thinking Positively	Page 291
• Self-Esteem	Wishes	Page 308

ADDITIONAL PROBLEMS FOR WHICH THIS EXERCISE MAY BE USEFUL

- Depression
- Self-Esteem
- Separation Anxiety
- Specific Phobia

SUGGESTIONS FOR PROCESSING THIS EXERCISE WITH CLIENT

Young children frequently have difficulty expressing anxiety and fears. Helping the child to identify and verbally express fears can be therapeutic.

Instruct the child to think of a time when he/she was anxious. It may be helpful to have the child identify a specific time when he/she was anxious. The child will complete a drawing that focuses on this event and bring the drawing to the next therapy session.

By focusing on a specific event within the therapy session, the child can be encouraged to identify precipitants and fears as well as begin to recognize strategies for managing anxiety more effectively.

The therapy session can also be used to assess whether these fears are rational and begin to focus on evidence that contradicts these fears.

SEPARATION FEELINGS

Describe a time when you were anxious:

_____

_____

_____

Draw a picture of this event

STEPS TO INDEPENDENCE

GOALS OF THE EXERCISE

1. Increase the ability to tolerate separation from attachment figures without exhibiting heightened emotional distress, regressive behaviors, temper outbursts, or pleading.
2. Parents/guardian will establish and maintain appropriate parent-child boundaries and set firm, consistent limits when the client exhibits temper outbursts.
3. Increase the ability to manage separation from parents/guardian without displaying excessive emotional distress.

ADDITIONAL HOMEWORK THAT MAY BE APPLICABLE TO SEPARATION ANXIETY

• Anxiety	Coping with Anxiety	Page 45
• Anxiety	Unrealistic Fears	Page 51
• Anxiety	Managing Anxiety	Page 55
• Anxiety	Stress Management	Page 59
• Anxiety	Relaxation	Page 63
• Depression	Rewriting Cognitive Distortions	Page 130
• Self-Esteem	Thinking Positively	Page 291
• Self-Esteem	Wishes	Page 308

ADDITIONAL PROBLEMS FOR WHICH THIS EXERCISE MAY BE USEFUL

- Depression
- Self-Esteem
- Separation Anxiety
- Specific Phobia

SUGGESTIONS FOR PROCESSING THIS EXERCISE WITH CLIENT

For this assignment the therapist will be developing a reward system that reinforces the child for being able to manage separation from parents/guardian without displaying excessive emotional distress.

This assignment should be divided over several weeks and involves establishing a hierarchy of anxiety-provoking events. In the therapy session, review concepts associated with systematic desensitization. For this technique to be effective, the child will need to build upon successive successes. Therefore it is imperative to get an accurate picture of current fears. Instruct the child that he/she will need to list fears and will rate these fears from 1 to 5.

For the first step of this assignment, the child will identify anxiety-provoking situations. In the therapy session with both the child and the family, list 10 situations that are anxiety provoking for the child. Instruct the child that for homework he/she will have to rate each situation from 1 to 5, with 5 being the most anxiety provoking. Remind the child to bring the list to the next therapy session.

In the next session, review the list with the child and create a staircase of anxiety in which the least anxiety-provoking situation is on the bottom step and the most anxiety-provoking situation is at the top. Use therapy sessions to help the child develop strategies to manage the anxiety. Practice relaxation strategies in the therapy sessions. When the child is able to successfully complete the task on the first step, assign this task as homework. Each week the child will build upon previous successes and complete an assignment related to anxiety.

STEPS TO INDEPENDENCE

Rate the degree of anxiety you feel in each of the listed situations.

1 = little anxiety   3 = medium anxiety   5 = extreme anxiety

Situation	Anxiety Rating				
_____	1	2	3	4	5
_____	1	2	3	4	5
_____	1	2	3	4	5
_____	1	2	3	4	5
_____	1	2	3	4	5
_____	1	2	3	4	5
_____	1	2	3	4	5
_____	1	2	3	4	5
_____	1	2	3	4	5
_____	1	2	3	4	5

Anxiety Hierarchy

List anxiety-provoking situations on the lines provided, with the least anxiety-provoking situation listed on line 1 and the most anxiety-provoking situation on line 10. Cross off each task as it is completed.

10 _____

9 _____

8 _____

7 _____

6 _____

5 _____

4 _____

3 _____

2 _____

1 _____

Section XXIII

SEXUAL ABUSE

SURVIVOR

GOALS OF THE EXERCISE

1. Identify and express feelings connected with the abuse through drawings.
2. Verbally express the experience of the abuse.
3. Rebuild a sense of self-worth and remove the sense of fear, shame, and sadness.
4. Verbalize feelings associated with the abuse.

ADDITIONAL HOMEWORK THAT MAY BE APPLICABLE TO SEXUAL ABUSE

ADDITIONAL PROBLEMS FOR WHICH THIS EXERCISE MAY BE USEFUL

- Physical and Emotional Abuse
- PTSD

SUGGESTIONS FOR PROCESSING THIS EXERCISE WITH CLIENT

Sexual abuse can have long-term effects on a child's feeling of self-worth and on future relationships. It is imperative for the therapist to be respectful of the child's feelings and the child's pace for expressing the experience of abuse. Pressuring a child to express feelings can revictimize the child.

It is imperative that the therapist using this assignment have adequate experience working with children who have been sexually abused. Working outside of one's clinical expertise can be dangerous to the client and is unethical.

This assignment can help the skilled clinician to work with a child who has a history of sexual abuse. For this assignment the child will complete two drawings. The first drawing will depict the location where the abuse occurred. Instruct the child to draw a picture of the location where the abuse occurred.

The second drawing will be a picture of himself/herself before and after the abuse.

These drawings will help the child begin to verbalize feelings about the abuse in the therapy session. Instruct the child to complete the drawings and bring them to the therapy session. The drawings can be used to initiate discussion of feelings associated with the abuse.

The therapist should also use his/her best clinical judgment to determine whether this assignment should be completed in the session instead of as a homework assignment.

SURVIVOR

Draw a picture of the location where the abuse occurred.

Draw a picture of yourself before the abuse.

Draw a picture of yourself now.

MY LETTER

GOALS OF THE EXERCISE

1. Identify and express feelings connected with the abuse.
2. Verbally express the experience of the abuse.
3. Rebuild a sense of self-worth and remove the sense of fear, shame, and sadness.
4. Verbalize feelings associated with the abuse.

ADDITIONAL HOMEWORK THAT MAY BE APPLICABLE TO SEXUAL ABUSE

• Anger Management	Anger Control	Page 31
• Anger Management	Anger Management	Page 36
• Anxiety	Relaxation	Page 63
• Self-Esteem	Recognizing the Wonderful Things about You	Page 286
• Self-Esteem	Bill of Rights	Page 305
• Self-Esteem	Wishes	Page 308
• Physical and Emotional Abuse	My Experience	Page 248
• Physical and Emotional Abuse	Safety	Page 253
• PTSD	Impact	Page 259
• PTSD	Coping with Trauma	Page 264
• PTSD	What Happened?	Page 268

ADDITIONAL PROBLEMS FOR WHICH THIS EXERCISE MAY BE USEFUL

- Physical and Emotional Abuse
- PTSD

SUGGESTIONS FOR PROCESSING THIS EXERCISE WITH CLIENT

This assignment can help the skilled clinician to work with a child who has a history of sexual abuse. For this assignment the child will be asked to write a letter to the perpetrator of the abuse. This assignment can be extremely difficult for survivors of sexual abuse. Therefore, it is imperative that the therapist work very closely with the child. The therapist should also use his/her best clinical judgment to determine whether this assignment should be completed in the session instead of as a homework assignment.

In most situations this therapeutic activity should be completed within the session. It is imperative for the therapist to be respectful of the child's feelings and the child's pace for expressing the experience of abuse. Pressuring a child to express feelings can revictimize the child.

As with all areas of clinical work, it is important that the therapist have experience working with children who have been abused. Working outside of one's clinical expertise can be dangerous to the client and is unethical.

MY LETTER

Dear _____ ,

_____

_____

_____

_____

_____

_____

_____

_____

_____

_____

_____

_____

_____

_____

_____

_____

_____

_____

_____

_____

Section XXIV

SLEEP DISTURBANCE

SLEEP PATTERNS

GOALS OF THE EXERCISE

1. Increase the awareness of daily stressors.
2. Increase the awareness of sleep patterns.
3. Identify factors that may be disturbing sleep.

ADDITIONAL HOMEWORK THAT MAY BE APPLICABLE TO SLEEP DISTURBANCE

- Anxiety   Coping with Anxiety   Page 45
- Anxiety   Unrealistic Fears   Page 51
- Anxiety   Managing Anxiety   Page 55
- Anxiety   Stress Management   Page 59
- Anxiety   Relaxation   Page 63

ADDITIONAL PROBLEMS FOR WHICH THIS EXERCISE MAY BE USEFUL

- Anxiety
- Depression

SUGGESTIONS FOR PROCESSING THIS EXERCISE WITH CLIENT

This homework assignment is designed for parents/guardian and/or older children to identify factors that might be having an impact on sleep patterns. This assignment creates a log to document sleep patterns and daily events that might be affecting sleep.

In the therapy session, discuss factors that might be affecting sleep. Instruct the client that for this assignment the parents/guardian or child will be documenting patterns related to sleeping. This assignment will also be used to determine current sleep patterns and routines.

Review different types of stressors that might have an impact on sleep patterns—for example, watching disturbing movies, eating prior to sleeping, engaging in stressful activities, and worrying excessively. The parents/guardian or child will need to document stressors and different sleep patterns on the log sheet.

The parents/guardian or child will log the time of sleep preparations and bedtime. Wake-up times and naps will also be recorded. The log sheet should be completed each day. The parents/guardian and child should answer each question in the log each day. The completed log sheet should be brought to the next therapy session for review and discussion. This log sheet can be used to develop appropriate sleep routines and identify factors related to sleep disturbance.

SLEEP PATTERNS

SUNDAY

Wake-up time _____   Amount of sleep during the day _____

Daily stressors _____

Time of start of bedtime routine (putting on pajamas, brushing teeth) _____

Time in bed _____   Time fell asleep _____

MONDAY

Wake-up time _____   Amount of sleep during the day _____

Daily stressors _____

Time of start of bedtime routine (putting on pajamas, brushing teeth) _____

Time in bed _____   Time fell asleep _____

TUESDAY

Wake-up time _____   Amount of sleep during the day _____

Daily stressors _____

Time of start of bedtime routine (putting on pajamas, brushing teeth) _____

Time in bed _____   Time fell asleep _____

WEDNESDAY

Wake-up time _____   Amount of sleep during the day _____

Daily stressors _____

Time of start of bedtime routine (putting on pajamas, brushing teeth) _____

Time in bed _____   Time fell asleep _____

THURSDAY

Wake-up time _____   Amount of sleep during the day _____

Daily stressors _____

Time of start of bedtime routine (putting on pajamas, brushing teeth) _____

Time in bed _____   Time fell asleep _____

FRIDAY

Wake-up time _____   Amount of sleep during the day _____

Daily stressors _____

Time of start of bedtime routine (putting on pajamas, brushing teeth) _____

Time in bed _____   Time fell asleep _____

SATURDAY

Wake-up time _____   Amount of sleep during the day _____

Daily stressors _____

Time of start of bedtime routine (putting on pajamas, brushing teeth) _____

Time in bed _____   Time fell asleep _____

SLEEP ROUTINE

GOALS OF THE EXERCISE

1. Increase the awareness of sleep patterns.
2. Establish a regular bedtime routine.
3. Decrease factors that can disturb sleep.

ADDITIONAL HOMEWORK THAT MAY BE APPLICABLE TO SLEEP DISTURBANCE

ADDITIONAL PROBLEMS FOR WHICH THIS EXERCISE MAY BE USEFUL

- Anxiety
- Depression

SUGGESTIONS FOR PROCESSING THIS EXERCISE WITH CLIENT

This exercise follows the previous exercise, "Sleep Patterns," which identifies factors that have an impact on sleep. Once these factors have been identified, therapy can begin to focus on strategies to establish regular sleep routines.

Frequently simply establishing a routine can aid in decreasing sleep disturbances. In the therapy session, review the worksheet with both the child and the parents/guardian. Emphasize the importance of establishing a routine for bedtime.

For homework, the child, with the assistance of his/her parents/guardian, will complete the bottom of this worksheet, which asks for a description of the child's routine. The parents/guardian and child should describe the steps included in the child's bedtime routine.

The parents/guardian and child create a five-step bedtime routine. All preparations for bedtime should be included in the routine (taking a bath, putting on pajamas, brushing teeth, etc.).

In discussing issues with the parents/guardian, be respectful of the fact that there are times when routine must be broken. However, in general it is best to try to maintain the bedtime routine.

For the next part of this assignment, the child and/or parents/guardian will record weekly sleep patterns. The weekly schedule will monitor wake-up time, bedtime, and any difficulties during the week.

SLEEP ROUTINE

Establishing a Routine

Children respond well to schedules and routines. Therefore, it is important to establish a daily routine for your child. It is particularly helpful to establish routines for meals, the morning, and bedtime.

A typical bedtime routine might include brushing teeth, washing up, putting on pajamas, reading a book, and lights out. The exact details of the routine are not important; the consistency of this routine is the issue.

Map Out Your Child's Bedtime Routine

Describe the steps of your nighttime routine.

Step 1 →

Step 2 →

Step 3 →

Step 4 →

Step 5 →

Sleep Log

SUNDAY

Wake-up time _____

Time of start of bedtime routine _____

Time in bed _____   Time fell asleep _____

MONDAY

Wake-up time _____

Time of start of bedtime routine _____

Time in bed _____   Time fell asleep _____

TUESDAY

Wake-up time _____

Time of start of bedtime routine _____

Time in bed _____   Time fell asleep _____

WEDNESDAY

Wake-up time _____

Time of start of bedtime routine _____

Time in bed _____   Time fell asleep _____

THURSDAY

Wake-up time _____

Time of start of bedtime routine _____

Time in bed _____   Time fell asleep _____

FRIDAY

Wake-up time _____

Time of start of bedtime routine _____

Time in bed _____   Time fell asleep _____

_____

SATURDAY

Wake-up time _____

Time of start of bedtime routine _____

Time in bed _____   Time fell asleep _____

_____

Section XXV

SOCIAL PHOBIA

MAKING FRIENDS

GOALS OF THE EXERCISE

1. Increase social contacts.
2. Increase positive feelings associated with social interactions.
3. Increase participation in interpersonal and peer group activities.

ADDITIONAL HOMEWORK THAT MAY BE APPLICABLE TO SOCIAL PHOBIA

• Anxiety	Coping with Anxiety	Page 45
• Anxiety	Stress Management	Page 59
• Anxiety	Relaxation	Page 63
• Depression	What Makes You Happy?	Page 121
• Self-Esteem	Goal Setting	Page 313
• Separation Anxiety	Fun with Friends	Page 322

ADDITIONAL PROBLEMS FOR WHICH THIS EXERCISE MAY BE USEFUL

- Anxiety
- Self-Esteem
- Separation Anxiety

SUGGESTIONS FOR PROCESSING THIS EXERCISE WITH CLIENT

This assignment is designed for the child who is resistant to initiating peer interactions. For this assignment, the child will be encouraged to focus on strategies to develop peer relationships.

Review the homework assignment in the therapy session. For the first section of this assignment, the child will draw pictures of a variety of strategies that can be used to develop peer relationships. Review each strategy in the therapy session, and instruct the child that he/she will need to complete a drawing for each strategy.

For the second section of this assignment, the child will review a short list of strategies that can be used to initiate an interaction with a peer. Review each of these strategies in the session and instruct the child that he/she will need to use one strategy this week to initiate a peer interaction.

In the therapy session, identify the peer with whom the client will be interacting. On the bottom of this worksheet, the child is instructed to draw a picture illustrating the strategy used.

Review the completed assignment in the next therapy session. The child can continue this assignment several times with different peers and/or using different strategies. For this assignment to be effective, it is critical for the peer interaction to be positive.

MAKING FRIENDS

Draw a picture of yourself using each of these strategies to make a friend.

Smiling	Listening
Introducing yourself	**Inviting someone to do something fun**
Giving a compliment	**Joining a club**

There are lots of ways to make friends. Here are some suggestions for how you can make new friends and keep old friends.

Start a conversation   Listen

Play a game   Join a group

Tell a joke   Do not criticize

Give a compliment   Keep a secret

Don't put others down   Don't gossip

Talk about something you both like

List another way you can make a friend:

_____

Draw a picture of the strategy you used this week.

FRIENDS

GOALS OF THE EXERCISE

1. Increase social contacts.
2. Increase positive feelings associated with social interactions.
3. Increase participation in interpersonal and peer group activities.

ADDITIONAL HOMEWORK THAT MAY BE APPLICABLE TO SOCIAL PHOBIA

• Anxiety	Coping with Anxiety	Page 45
• Anxiety	Stress Management	Page 59
• Anxiety	Relaxation	Page 63
• Depression	What Makes You Happy?	Page 121
• Self-Esteem	Goal Setting	Page 313
• Separation Anxiety	Fun with Friends	Page 322

ADDITIONAL PROBLEMS FOR WHICH THIS EXERCISE MAY BE USEFUL

- Anxiety
- Self-Esteem
- Separation Anxiety

SUGGESTIONS FOR PROCESSING THIS EXERCISE WITH CLIENT

This assignment is designed for the child who is shy and resistant to developing peer relationships. The main goal of this assignment is to help the child identify positive aspects of peer relationships.

The two sections of this assignment can be completed in one week or over several weeks. Review the assignment with the child in the therapy session.

For the first section, the child will need to list 10 qualities of a good friend and describe how he/she can be a good friend. If the child has difficulty writing responses, he/she can get help from an adult.

The next section of this assignment focuses more closely on developing peer relationships. The child will identify statements that can be used to initiate peer contacts. Review the instructions with the child. First, the child will need to list statements that can be used to start a conversation with a peer. Next, the child will need to use three of these statements in the following week. Instruct the child to color in the statements that he/she used during the week.

FRIENDS

Describe 10 characteristics or qualities of a good friend.

1. _____

2. _____

3. _____

4. _____

5. _____

6. _____

7. _____

8. _____

9. _____

10. _____

Describe how you could be a good friend.

_____

_____

_____

_____

_____

In each of the bubbles write the words that you can use to start a conversation with a friend.

This week, use three of these statements at least once. Color in the statements that you use this week.

SOCIAL PHOBIA

GOALS OF THE EXERCISE

1. Explore social situations in which the client interacts with peers without excessive fear or anxiety.
2. Reduce the anxiety associated with social situations.
3. Express feelings associated with unfamiliar people or when placed in new social situations.

ADDITIONAL HOMEWORK THAT MAY BE APPLICABLE TO SOCIAL PHOBIA

• Anxiety	Coping with Anxiety	Page 45
• Anxiety	Stress Management	Page 59
• Anxiety	Relaxation	Page 63
• Depression	What Makes You Happy?	Page 121
• Self-Esteem	Goal Setting	Page 313
• Separation Anxiety	Fun with Friends	Page 322

ADDITIONAL PROBLEMS FOR WHICH THIS EXERCISE MAY BE USEFUL

- Anxiety
- Self-Esteem
- Separation Anxiety

SUGGESTIONS FOR PROCESSING THIS EXERCISE WITH CLIENT

Children with social phobia frequently experience excessive anxiety in social situations. The past experience of anxiety can inhibit social interactions, whereby the child recalls previous feelings of anxiety and refrains from initiating contact with peers.

This assignment can help the child identify positive social interactions. The first part of this assignment encourages the child to identify social situations in which he/she interacts with peers and does not report anxiety. In the therapy session, identify one positive peer social interaction in which the child can participate during the week. The child will draw a picture about this social interaction.

In the therapy session, explore aspects of this situation that differ from other social situations (for example, the person, the activity).

In the therapy session, help the child identify social situations that are anxiety provoking. Together create a list of anxiety-provoking social situations. The child will rate these situations from 1 to 5 as a homework assignment. Remind the child to bring the list to the next therapy session.

In the next session, review the list with the child and create a hierarchy of anxiety from the least anxiety-provoking situation to the most anxiety-provoking situation.

Use therapy sessions to help the child develop strategies to manage the anxiety. Practice relaxation strategies in the therapy session. When the child is able to successfully complete the first task as a homework assignment, move on to the next task. Each week the child will build upon previous successes and complete a social task.

SOCIAL PHOBIA

Think of a fun time that you have had with a friend. Draw a picture of you and your friend.

Rate the degree of anxiety you feel in each of these social situations.

1 = little anxiety   3 = medium anxiety   5 = extreme anxiety

Social Situation	Anxiety Rating				
_____	1	2	3	4	5
_____	1	2	3	4	5
_____	1	2	3	4	5
_____	1	2	3	4	5
_____	1	2	3	4	5
_____	1	2	3	4	5
_____	1	2	3	4	5
_____	1	2	3	4	5
_____	1	2	3	4	5
_____	1	2	3	4	5

Anxiety Hierarchy

List anxiety-provoking situations on the following lines, with the least anxiety-provoking situation listed on line 1 and the most anxiety-provoking situation on line 10. Cross off each task as it is completed.

Task	Date Completed
1. _____	_____
2. _____	_____
3. _____	_____
4. _____	_____
5. _____	_____
6. _____	_____
7. _____	_____
8. _____	_____
9. _____	_____
10. _____	_____

COMMUNICATION

GOALS OF THE EXERCISE

1. Increase assertive communication to deal more effectively with peers.
2. Teach assertive communication skills.

ADDITIONAL HOMEWORK THAT MAY BE APPLICABLE TO SOCIAL PHOBIA

- Anxiety   Coping with Anxiety   Page 45
- Anxiety   Stress Management   Page 59
- Anxiety   Relaxation   Page 63
- Depression   What Makes You Happy?   Page 121
- Self-Esteem   Goal Setting   Page 313
- Separation Anxiety   Fun with Friends   Page 322

ADDITIONAL PROBLEMS FOR WHICH THIS EXERCISE MAY BE USEFUL

- Anxiety
- Self-Esteem
- Separation Anxiety

SUGGESTIONS FOR PROCESSING THIS EXERCISE WITH CLIENT

Children who have difficulties with peer relationships are sometimes reluctant to communicate their feelings and thoughts because they fear criticism from their peers. This fear can often lead to withdrawal from peer relationships. Often these children do not assertively communicate and therefore their peers do not know their opinions, likes, or dislikes.

This assignment will help the child begin to communicate assertively with his/her peers. In the therapy session, provide an overview of assertive, aggressive, and passive communication styles. Use role-plays to help the child practice each communication style. Be certain to focus on both nonverbal and verbal communication.

Review the sample item in the therapy session. Be certain that the child has a clear understanding of assertive, aggressive, and passive responses.

For the homework assignment, describe a peer situation in which the child sometimes has difficulty. Write a brief description of the situation in the top section of the worksheet. For this assignment, the child will have to identify passive, assertive, and aggressive responses to each situation. In the therapy session, review the situation and role-play responses.

COMMUNICATION

Situation: A friend asks you to play baseball, but you really don't like baseball.

Describe an aggressive response to this situation:

Describe a passive response to this situation:

Describe an assertive response to this situation:

Situation:

Describe an aggressive response to this situation:

Describe a passive response to this situation:

Describe an assertive response to this situation:

Section XXVI

SPECIFIC PHOBIA

OVERCOMING FEARS

GOALS OF THE EXERCISE

1. Verbalize the cognitive beliefs and messages that mediate the anxiety response.
2. Revise distorted core schemas that trigger negative self-talk.

ADDITIONAL HOMEWORK THAT MAY BE APPLICABLE TO SPECIFIC PHOBIA

- Anxiety   Coping with Anxiety   Page 45
- Anxiety   Unrealistic Fears   Page 51
- Anxiety   Managing Anxiety   Page 55
- Anxiety   Stress Management   Page 59
- Anxiety   Relaxation   Page 63

ADDITIONAL PROBLEMS FOR WHICH THIS EXERCISE MAY BE USEFUL

- Anxiety
- Depression
- Self-Esteem

SUGGESTIONS FOR PROCESSING THIS EXERCISE WITH CLIENT

Children with a history of anxiety frequently have irrational fears in response to many situations. For example, the child who is afraid of dogs might fear that a dog will bite him/her, despite the fact that he/she has never been bitten. This assignment is designed for children who have distorted schemas and irrational fears. A major goal of treatment is to teach the client to challenge cognitive distortions and to increase positive self-talk.

This homework assignment should be used only when the therapist has first provided education about cognitive distortions. The child and family should be educated about cognitive theory and strategies for challenging cognitive distortions. This assignment is designed for older children and adolescents. Young children will have difficulty with this assignment.

This assignment can aid the child in identifying and challenging irrational beliefs. Instruct the child that for each situation he/she will have to identify three alternative interpretations for anxiety situations. Review the sample in the therapy session. Instruct the child that he/she will have to complete a similar worksheet for homework. Complete the top line of the worksheet in the therapy session by describing the child's fear and typical reaction. For homework the child will have to identify three alternative interpretations for the situation.

OVERCOMING FEARS

Sometimes when Janie sees a dog she thinks:

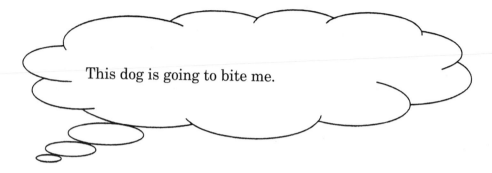

This dog is going to bite me.

Instead, she might think:

Sometimes when I _____ , I think:

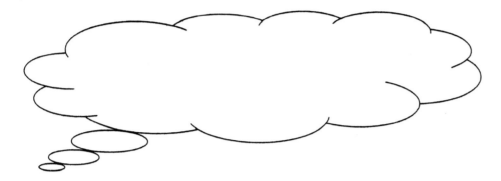

Instead, I might think:

NOT AFRAID ANYMORE

GOALS OF THE EXERCISE

1. Construct a hierarchy of situations that evoke increasing anxiety.
2. Learn how to use progressive relaxation techniques to manage anxiety.
3. Engage in feared behavior and experience anxiety.

ADDITIONAL HOMEWORK THAT MAY BE APPLICABLE TO SPECIFIC PHOBIA

• Anxiety	Coping with Anxiety	Page 45
• Anxiety	Unrealistic Fears	Page 51
• Anxiety	Managing Anxiety	Page 55
• Anxiety	Stress Management	Page 59
• Anxiety	Relaxation	Page 63

ADDITIONAL PROBLEMS FOR WHICH THIS EXERCISE MAY BE USEFUL

- Anxiety
- Depression
- Self-Esteem

SUGGESTIONS FOR PROCESSING THIS EXERCISE WITH CLIENT

This homework assignment uses the technique of systematic desensitization to help the child begin to decrease the level of anxiety. Because this process can be difficult for children to comprehend, it is important to include parents/guardian in both the therapy and the homework process. Additionally, parents/guardian often inadvertently reinforce the anxiety response.

This technique is most effective when the therapist has a clear understanding of the phobia and the anxiety response. In the therapy session, help the child identify situations that are anxiety provoking. Together create a list of anxiety-provoking situations. The child will rate these situations from 1 to 5 as a homework assignment. Instruct the child that he/she will have to rate the degree of anxiety by coloring in the amount of anxiety experienced on the graph.

Instruct the child to complete the assignment and bring it to the next session. Review the completed worksheet and copy the items on the anxiety goal sheet, ranging from the least anxiety-provoking situation to the most.

Use therapy sessions to help the child develop strategies to manage the anxiety. Practice relaxation strategies in the therapy sessions. When the child is able to successfully complete the first task as a homework assignment, move on to the next task. Each week the child will build upon previous successes and complete a task related to decreasing anxiety.

NOT AFRAID ANYMORE

On the left side of this sheet, list situations in which you feel anxious. On the right side, indicate the degree of anxiety you experience in each situation.

1 = little anxiety   3 = medium anxiety   5 = extreme anxiety

Situation	Color in the amount of anxiety.
_____	1 → 2 → 3 → 4 → 5
_____	1 → 2 → 3 → 4 → 5
_____	1 → 2 → 3 → 4 → 5
_____	1 → 2 → 3 → 4 → 5
_____	1 → 2 → 3 → 4 → 5
_____	1 → 2 → 3 → 4 → 5
_____	1 → 2 → 3 → 4 → 5
_____	1 → 2 → 3 → 4 → 5

Task List

Situations (listed from least anxiety provoking to most anxiety provoking)	Date Completed
1. _____	_____
2. _____	_____
3. _____	_____
4. _____	_____
5. _____	_____
6. _____	_____
7. _____	_____
8. _____	_____
9. _____	_____
10. _____	_____

ABOUT THE CD-ROM

INTRODUCTION

The forms on the enclosed CD-ROM are saved in Microsoft Word for Windows version 7.0. In order to use the forms, you will need to have word processing software capable of reading Microsoft Word for Windows version 7.0 files.

SYSTEM REQUIREMENTS

- IBM PC or compatible computer
- CD-ROM drive
- Windows 95 or later
- Microsoft Word for Windows version 7.0 (including the Microsoft converter*) or later or other word processing software capable of reading Microsoft Word for Windows 7.0 files.

  *Word 7.0 needs the Microsoft converter file installed in order to view and edit all enclosed files. If you have trouble viewing the files, download the free converter from the Microsoft web site. The URL for the converter is:
  http://office.microsoft.com/downloads/2000/wrd97cnv.aspx

  Microsoft also has a viewer that can be downloaded, which allows you to view, but not edit documents. This viewer can be downloaded at:
  http://office.microsoft.com/downloads/9798/wdvw9716.aspx

Note: Many popular word processing programs are capable of reading Microsoft Word for Windows 7.0 files. However, users should be aware that a slight amount of formatting might be lost when using a program other than Microsoft Word. If your word processor cannot read Microsoft Word for Windows 7.0 files, unformatted text files have been provided in the TXT directory on the CD-ROM.

HOW TO INSTALL THE FILES ONTO YOUR COMPUTER

To install the files follow these instructions:

1. Insert the enclosed CD-ROM into the CD-ROM drive of your computer.
2. From the Start Menu, choose **Run.**
3. Type **D:\SETUP** and press **OK. (D:** represents the letter of your CD-ROM drive.)

4. The opening screen of the installation program will appear. Press **OK** to continue.
5. The default destination directory is `C:\SUFLERHW`. If you wish to change the default destination, you may do so now.
6. Press **OK** to continue. The installation program will copy all files to your hard drive in the `C:\SUFLERHW` or user-designated directory.

USING THE FILES

Loading Files

To use the word processing files, launch your word processing program. Select **File, Open** from the pull-down menu. Select the appropriate drive and directory. If you installed the files to the default directory, the files will be located in the `C:\SUFLERHW` directory. A list of files should appear. If you do not see a list of files in the directory, you need to select **WORD DOCUMENT (*.DOC)** under **Files of Type**. Double-click on the file you want to open. Edit the file according to your needs.

Printing Files

If you want to print the files, select **File, Print** from the pull-down menu.

Saving Files

When you have finished editing a file, you should save it under a new file name by selecting **File, Save As** from the pull-down menu.

USER ASSISTANCE

If you need assistance with installation or if you have a damaged CD-ROM, please contact Wiley Technical Support at:

Phone: (201) 748-6753
Fax: (201) 748-6540 (Attention: Wiley Technical Support)
URL: www.wiley.com/techsupport

To place additional orders or to request information about other Wiley products, please call (800) 225-5945.

For information about the CD-ROM see the **About the CD-ROM** section on page 375.

WILEY
Publishers Since 1807